Assessing Impact

Evidence and Action

Ellen Earle Chaffee

Peter T. Ewell

Sherril B. Gelmon

George Kuh

Theodore J. Marchese

Margaret A. Miller

Grant Wiggins

Presentations from the
1997 AAHE Conference on Assessment & Quality

Ordering Information
Additional copies of this publication can be purchased by contacting:
American Association for Higher Education
One Dupont Circle, Suite 360
Washington, DC 20036-1110
202/293-6440 x11, fax 202/293-0073
www.aahe.org

ISBN 1-56377-026-1

Contents
Assessing Impact: Evidence and Action

Foreword
....
Assessing Impact: Evidence and Action

When I hear an excellent presentation at a conference, I often long for a written record of the talk. I want the exact quote that I couldn't write fast enough to capture or the apt example that crystallized a concept. Although handouts can help, I want a fuller, more permanent reference. Since I can't hear all featured speeches in the same time slot, written versions of those I haven't heard are also valuable.

This collection from the 1997 AAHE Conference on Assessment & Quality is designed to fill the bill for those of us who want to benefit over time from the ideas of prominent speakers. Three plenary presentations and four introductions to program strands are included in this publication. As we rely on him to do so well, Peter Ewell surveys the national landscape in "Accountability and Assessment in a Second Decade: New Looks or Same Old Story?" Watch for his three imperatives for current action: defining the academic integrity of the degree, identifying core processes related to the degree, and focusing on each institution's own quality assurance and improvement processes. You can learn about ideas of AAHE's new president, Margaret Miller, by reading "Looking for Results: The Second Decade." She challenges us all to pay attention to tracking students' deep learning, understanding the effects of powerful pedagogies on students and teachers, addressing public questions and concerns, establishing standards, and examining the effects of technology on assessment and vice versa. Grant Wiggins differentiates between evaluation and the most necessary component of assessment in his presentation "Feedback: How Learning Occurs." Those of you who like narrative evidence will especially enjoy his talk.

The four introductions to thematic strands of the conference focus on different aspects of the conference's attention to the impact of assessment. With a dramatic introduction about her campus's active response to the flooding crisis in her state, Ellen Chaffee demonstrates that campus environments based on feedback and assessment are flexible and ready to serve student and societal needs. Sherril Gelmon reconceptualizes accreditation based on assessment as an opportunity to improve. George Kuh challenges faculty members and student affairs staff to tighten connections between the curriculum and students' out-of-class experiences. In a talk that focuses on the central reason for doing assessment, Ted Marchese links the latest findings about how people learn to the design and assessment of experiences that prompt deep learning.

I hope that you will provide feedback to the speakers represented in this book. Presenters were encouraged to keep their talks in the form presented rather than turning them into articles, so you will hear their voices loudly and clearly in this volume. They will be pleased to hear back from you about your ideas concerning their topics.

As always, the AAHE Assessment Forum welcomes your ideas about how it can serve your needs. I am convinced that this collection is one such way and invite you to learn from and enjoy these seven stimulating presentations.

Barbara L. Cambridge
Director, AAHE Assessment Forum
American Association for Higher Education

W e have had numerous, exciting sessions at this conference that demonstrate the power of assessment to help stimulate instructional improvement. But we must always remember that the roots of the movement have always been planted firmly in two, quite different traditions. One was a

Accountability and Assessment in a Second Decade
New Looks or Same Old Story?

BY PETER T. EWELL

series of curricular-reform efforts emerging from the academy itself, which first became apparent in the late seventies and early eighties and was signalled unmistakably as a presence by such reports as NIE's *Involvement in Learning* and AAC&U's *Integrity in the College Curriculum*. The other arose out of a complex of political forces — largely at the state level and closely bound up with the reform of K-12 education — best marked by the publication of the National Governors Association's report *Time for Results* in 1986. Ever since, assessment, as a movement, has harbored a latent contradiction, producing a strange dance between external policy requirements and internal faculty consciousness.

The dynamic produced by this contradiction has been occasionally beneficial and at times highly acerbic. On the one hand, it is probably fair to say that external pressure largely started the conversation in the first place. Many of you may remember the first National Assessment Forum, jointly sponsored by AAHE and NIE and held in Columbia, South Carolina, in 1985, which drew almost twice as many attendees than initially anticipated — largely due to fears of what assessment might "do to" them. Others may recall some of the earliest instances of state action in this arena, occurring in places like Virginia, Colorado, and Missouri. It is no coincidence, I believe, that some of the most creative, faculty-centered, and forward-looking examples of assessment practice — apparent both in this conference's program and elsewhere — came out of institutions in

But it is also fair to say that political action has not been applied gently and that, in many cases, it has succeeded in strongly alienating faculty from the kinds of long-term participatory processes that are really needed.

• •

states like these, which had early assessment mandates. Such examples can rightly be claimed as a significant success for state policy. Just the same role, in fact, is now being played by regional accrediting agencies — though a bit later, perhaps, than both national and state policymakers would have liked. Indeed, the actions of accreditors are stimulating interest in assessment on the part of a whole new crop of institutions — for the most part private and relatively prestigious — which have been able to sit out the movement up to now. So, on the whole, the role of external stimulation can be claimed in part to be salutary.

But it is also fair to say that political action has not been applied gently and that, in many cases, it has succeeded in strongly alienating faculty from the kinds of long-term participatory processes that are really needed. The dynamic here is also familiar, beginning with the fact that resistance is the first and most natural reaction of the academy to *any* external action. Resistance, in turn, has frequently resulted in escalating government counter-pressure — growing more marked during the period 1990-1994 as states entered a period of fiscal strain, and punctuated with both latent anti-intellectualism and impatience at the perceived inability of higher education to effectively police itself.

The relationship between assessment and accountability has thus always been rich and strange, conditioned by both the character of the surrounding politics and of changes within higher education itself. At times, political actors have been highly visionary — seeing higher education as a key to the nation's future and assessment as a needed internal tool for continually renewing its role as a national

asset. But at times, they have been dominated by a logic of retrenchment and disinvestment — seeing higher education as a costly and a privileged sector, with assessment an ideal vehicle for applying the needed discipline. In parallel, higher education's leaders have sometimes been able to use external mandates as levers for important internal changes. Time and again, in my work with campuses during the mid to late eighties, for instance, provosts and presidents would inform me of the sublime utility of being able to blame on somebody else the impetus for changes that they themselves wanted to accomplish. But on other occasions, higher education's leaders have seen assessment as deeply threatening to the historic values of academic freedom and institutional autonomy and, as a consequence, as something to be resisted at all costs.

This shifting relationship has been played out on many levels during the past decade, and you can be forgiven for not remembering the details. The ups and downs of initiatives such as the SPRE (State Postsecondary Review Entities), the National Policy Board for Institutional Accreditation (NPB), the National Education Goals process, New Jersey's College Outcomes Evaluation Program (COEP), Colorado's Higher Education Accountability Act, Ohio's Selective Excellence program, or three successive waves of mandate in South Carolina must seem like distant rumbles to you who actually *do* the productive work of assessment. But they have influenced profoundly the issues we are asked to engage and, therefore, the actual procedures we have evolved in response.

My job this morning is to broadly review some of these implications and, as best I can, to foresee their future. This is, I confess, a daunting task. First, my own role in all of this is increasingly "right in the middle" — advising states and accreditors on evolving assessment and accountability policy, and participating in some of the few national-level conversations about assessment-as-accountability that still survive. As a result, I confess freely to a bias of particularism. Indeed, my own perceptions have undoubtedly been shaped decisively by the specific individual conversations and projects in which I have recently participated. But the "particulars" these days are also more important than ever. On the one hand, approaches to state policy have become highly fragmented, and individual states are going in vastly different directions. For striking examples, one has only to look to the arena of system governance. In places like New York, for example, we are witnessing the incipient breakup of one of the oldest and most centralized public systems of higher education in the nation; in Minnesota, in contrast, policymakers are busily creating a "super system" by merging all public institutions except the land-grant university. Rapid change is also apparent in the constant turnover of key personnel. Term limits and the tides of politics have generated a shifting and continually threatened cast of characters who must make the policies that affect us. To parody Hobbes, the lives of both legislators and SHEEOs have become increasingly "solitary, poor, nasty, brutish, and short."

Taken together, these forces make the job of forecasting a little like trying to chart the course of a deep ocean current in the middle of a hurricane. You are convinced that it is down there somewhere and conforming to an underlying pattern. But exceptionally strong local forces both block observation and compel you to spend most of your energy merely reacting to each wave in turn. Nevertheless, I will give the task a try by considering three main topics.

The first addresses the "deep background" for our current accountability situation. Here, I'd like to reflect a bit on the peculiar course of evolution that accountability in higher education has taken during the past two decades and argue that, at the most basic level, its fluctuations have been governed by some changing conceptions of the public purposes of higher education. One such shift in public purposes gave birth to what we now recognize as the assessment movement of the early eighties. And I believe that we are, at the moment, right in the middle of another one with partially unknown, but certainly significant, consequences for assessment.

Second, I'd like to offer some more direct and particular observations about several of the most apparent, near-term manifestations of assessment-as-accountability that many of you are facing right now and that I think will increasingly be with us all. These include, most prominently, growing linkages between assessed results and resource allocations (most obvious in the form of "performance funding"); growing "consumerism" and its demand for information about institutional performance in easily digestible form; and the gradual emergence of new (and more aggressive) institutional accreditation practices.

Finally, echoing Lee Knefelkamp's remarks in the opening plenary of this conference, I'd like to make a plea for collective action. To put it simply, I believe strongly that we have reached an important turning point in the meaning of public accountability for higher education, largely because narrow conceptions of accountability based on government regulation are breaking down everywhere. Despite political instability and occasional government nastiness, I believe, this broader situation means that we in the academy actually have a fairly good opportunity to put our own self-regulatory house in order. At the most basic level, this means taking a hard look at how we can remake processes of peer review to meet new circumstances and adopt deeper and more apparent levels of collective responsibility for the outcomes we produce. As yet, I think, we have not exploited this opportunity as we should have. As a result, we find ourselves somewhat in the circumstances so eloquently noted by Tocqueville in his introduction to *Democracy in America*, when describing the changing political conditions then occurring in Europe:

> Thus we have abandoned whatever
> good things the old order of society

could provide, but have not profited from what our present state can offer... and settling down complacently in the ruins of the old building, we seem to want to stay like that forever.

THE ROOTS OF OUR CURRENT CONDITION

Let me begin with the promised deep background by reviewing the evolving basis of accountability for higher education during the past two decades and its consequent implications for assessment. This relatively short period, I believe, has been unusually active in defining and redefining the relationship between higher education and the wider society. It has also been one in which higher education has, to an unusual degree, been redefining itself in reaction to new student clienteles and new modes of instructional delivery. Looking at the behavior of external forces during this period, I believe that most of what has occurred can be explained in terms of two major conceptual shifts in the underlying public purposes of higher education, both of which have had a substantial impact on the substance of accountability. Rather than fully supplanting each other, though, their effects have been like those of most social movements: new ideas have been layered into old ones in successive requirements. This is one reason why the current accountability picture is so complicated. It contains both new elements and forms that survive from an earlier period.

The first shift in conceptions of public purpose emerged in the early eighties and gave birth to the public side of assessment. As you may recall, the beginning of this period was characterized by a reasonably well established, liberal-democratic paradigm for higher education policy — forged in the mid-sixties as part of the original "Great Society" programs and embodied in the Higher Education Act of 1965. In essence, this policy paradigm saw higher education as a kind of "public utility"

— an enterprise intended primarily to provide benefits to individual citizens in the form of enhanced income and greater social mobility. The principal "public" role in this conception was to ensure equitable access to these largely individual benefits by expanding capacity and by providing direct financial assistance to those in need. By the early eighties, championed for the most part by an active and vocal group of governors, we began to see a somewhat different policy paradigm emerging. This conception of public purposes, which can be usefully termed the "corporatist" vision of higher education policy, rested instead on a view of higher education as a directed *collective investment,* with payoffs visible not only to individual citizens, but at the societal level as well in the form of economic growth and workforce competitiveness.

This corporatist conception of public purposes provided the basis for what was at the time some very substantial investment. But it also shifted markedly the terms of accountability. Instead of simply asking how higher education did its business and for whom — questions prompting the twin pillars of accountability of "efficiency and access" in the sixties and seventies — public policymakers were now interested in *what was produced* as a result. This conception permeated the NGA *Time for Results* report, issued in 1986, and largely stimulated the first set of state assessment mandates. At the time, it was broadly nonpartisan in character — championed both by Republican governors such as Tom Kean in New Jersey and John Ashcroft in Missouri, and by Democrats such as Roy Romer in Colorado. This vision was also heavily supported by higher education's own leaders because of the increased funding that might potentially result (though it was unclear at the time the degree to which they perceived the real implications of being judged on the basis of results). However constructed, the corporatist vision demanded an explicitly *public* role for higher education — one that required a new and proactive kind of policy consciousness. Writing from a broadly similar corporatist perspective of the proper relationship between government and other social institutions cast more than three hundred years ago, Hobbes spoke of the "Leviathan's" challenge to the then current Academy:

> It is therefore manifest that the instruction of the people depends wholly on the right teaching of youth in the Universities. But are not, may some men say, the Universities already learned enough to know how to do that? Or is it you will undertake to teach the Universities? Hard questions.

"Hard questions" indeed, but "teaching the universities" how to act more effectively as public servants was nevertheless a major feature of higher education policy during the mid to late eighties. Emerging from this proactive challenge were, in fact, three distinct manifestations of the corporatist policy vision.

Perhaps the most familiar was a range of state mandates that left public colleges and universities scrambling to develop assessment capacity. This was precisely the stimulus that, for better or worse, drove the bulk of early attention to assessment, and institutional behavior in the early years was almost entirely reactive as a result. But in retrospect, early state mandates were relatively nondirective in character — consistent with new corporate thinking about how to manage effectively by setting broad outcomes-related goals and allowing local managers substantial freedom in how they managed resources to achieve them. Early assessment mandates in states such as New Jersey, for instance, quite conspicuously embodied a "budget bargain" in which line-item budget controls on institutional expenditures were relaxed in return for the explicit adoption of an assessment program.

Often accompanying state assessment mandates as a second dimension of state action, though, was considerable investment in "quality improvement" through a myriad of

"Teaching the universities" how to act more effectively as public servants was nevertheless a major feature of higher education policy during the mid to late eighties.

● ●

addition-to-base funding schemes. Prominent examples included New Jersey's Governor's Challenge Grant program and Ohio's Selective Excellence program — as well as FIPSE at the national level — and many of these programs were used to explicitly finance assessment.

A third important manifestation emerged at the national level in the form of the National Education Goals, the first truly "national" conversation about educational outcomes in the United States. One prominent feature of the National Goals movement, of course, was the call to track progress on exiting college-student ability levels in such areas as communications and critical thinking.

These particular manifestations of the corporatist vision dominated the attention of many attending this conference during the period 1987-1992. By the early nineties, though, they were already beginning to unravel in the face of rising fiscal pressures. Hastening their demise in cost-conscious times was the all-too-apparent inability of the results of decentralized institution-specific assessment approaches to tell the public a coherent story about return on investment. But even this golden age of relatively nondirective state mandates set the stage for what was to follow by rendering *legitimate* in government hands two important policy tools. One was what proved to be an enduring tradition of government steering through alternative funding mechanisms. The second was the first real occasion for government to take a serious look at the *academic* business of colleges and universities — what they taught and how — in addition to simply how well they were managed. And both new roles were to emerge strongly when the political winds

Lacking any real knowledge about previous higher education policies, this new cast of characters is all too willing to "innovate" – sometimes radically – to achieve what they think needs to be accomplished.

● ●

shifted to the right.

A second shift in the perception of higher education's public purposes emerged in the period 1992-1994 and was certainly most apparent in the 1994 congressional elections. At its heart was a move back to the notion of a college education as primarily a private, individualized benefit, but with two quite different overtones that distinguished it from the earlier public utility model. One was the strong contention that, because individual citizens were the principal beneficiaries of higher education, they should be paying the bills as well. Coupled with fiscal pressure, this new ideology helped to fuel unprecedented increases in public tuition levels in many states. The second involved a dramatic reversal of established access and equity guarantees — for at least twenty-five years a bedrock value for both state and national higher education policy. This particular shift was, of course, most apparent in direct assaults on affirmative action in California and Texas. Above all, and in strong contrast to both the public utility and the corporatist visions, the resulting "New Right" public policy paradigm for the first time emphasized substantial *disinvestments* in higher education instead of ever-increasing levels of funding. More disturbing, it seemed to reflect widespread abandonment of the notion of higher education as an important collective asset.

Immediate impacts on the substance of accountability followed in turn and have become a prominent feature of the policy landscape for most public institutions. One is an increased emphasis on narrower definitions of results in the form of performance indicators — the majority of which now emphasize

efficiency over quality. Another is a growing emphasis on "consumer information" and "marketplace mechanisms" as a substitute for direct regulation — a theme strongly consistent with "reinventing government" and current corporate rhetoric. A final product is periodic calls for statewide outcomes testing in postsecondary education, though few states appear willing to invest the resources necessary to get this done.

As each of these examples makes clear, the kinds of assessment now being called for are directed toward *assuring quality* for external audiences far more than they are designed to induce local improvements in instructional practice. On the one hand, this reversion to pure quality assurance in government policy means that the game is clearer. Knowing that this is not "assessment" as we have come to understand it, we need to get on with the task of building more and better local evidence-gathering approaches in order to improve what we do in tight and uncertain circumstances — a motive consistent with the majority of sessions at this conference. On the other hand, this shift makes it imperative that we take back the initiative with respect to quality assurance itself by rebuilding once-credible approaches to peer review. Quality assurance for higher education is currently a respectable topic of debate in other countries — quite distinct from the improvement side of evaluation — and we need to join those nations in giving it the serious academic attention that it deserves.

A particular reason for doing so, moreover, are the core characteristics of those who have been thinking up the accountability measures that we increasingly have to face. The new wave of legislators and public board members appearing since 1994 are, for the most part, without prior experience. In the words of Edmund Burke, writing of the 1789 French Constituent Assemblies in *Reflections on the Revolution in France,* they are also individuals

who could not be expected to bear
with moderation or to conduct with

discretion a power which they themselves, more than any others, must be surprised to find in their hands.

Lacking any real knowledge about previous higher education policies, this new cast of characters is all too willing to "innovate" — sometimes radically — to achieve what they think needs to be accomplished. Few have any recollection of the many delicate negotiations that helped forge a workable consensus on state assessment policy in the mid to late eighties. In many states, moreover, term limits are exacerbating what is already an extremely limited experience base — rendering it even more difficult for states to evolve a coherent approach to higher education policy. No sooner is one set of requirements enacted than it is overturned by a new group of incumbents bent on leaving its own mark on the process.

One relatively stable set of characteristics in this new wave of elected officials and appointees, though, is their subscription to a particular set of values about education. Many have quite strong feelings about what ought to be taught and how. As such, their approach to higher education issues is often strongly at variance with the equally Republican corporatist view, which emphasizes the development of cross-cutting, higher-order intellectual skills as a foundation for improved productivity and workforce development. One important tenet of the New Right vision, for example, is a return to traditional disciplinary content in the form of Western civilization, American government and citizenship, and the classics of Western philosophy — often embodied in a call for a mid-fifties-style core curriculum. Another is strong rejection of the whole notion of remediation — partly on the basis of cost (resting on the contention that this is K-12's job and the public shouldn't have to pay for it twice) and partly on the basis of restricting admission only to those who should "appropriately" be going to college. In dealing with such individuals, it is important to recognize the particular terms and phrases that we in the academy may use in all inno-

cence and sincerity that can really set them off. As our colleagues in K-12 have learned to their dismay, one of them is "critical thinking" — a term that the radical right sees as teaching individuals to reject core cultural, religious, and patriotic fundamentals. Another is "global," which is seen from this perspective as evidence of a dangerous movement to undermine uniquely American perspectives and values. At the very least, therefore, we need to watch our language — if only to guard against unanticipated reactions to what we really mean to accomplish. More important, the increasing prominence of such rhetoric gives us a wake-up call about the core academic values that we need to actively protect in developing workable accountability alternatives.

This "new look" in higher education policy, it is important to emphasize, is by no means a done deal. The original foundations of the corporatist policy vision are still out there as strong as ever in many states, and this vision is noticeably embodied in federal policy initiatives like School-to-Work and the Clinton administration's tuition tax-credit proposals. As illustrated by the latter, moreover, surviving Democrats have joined midroad Republicans in emphasizing this policy perspective. Indeed, splits between its New Right and corporatist members in many states are causing difficult rifts in the Republican party itself — often played out in unpredictable and unusually contentious debates about policies affecting higher education. A revealing illustration is provided by a number of bills currently before state legislatures that would ban the use of Social Security numbers for research purposes — an action advanced on libertarian New Right grounds, but whose results would make it extremely difficult to carry on the kinds of workforce tracking and development studies that corporate folks say they need.

If all of this sounds confusing, that's because it is. At the state level, we really are in the middle of a period of considerable policy turmoil with no clear pattern dominant. At the federal level, in turn, we appear to have entered a "low-risk" policy phase — with debates about the upcoming reauthorization of the Higher Education Act likely to usher in something very like "business as usual" with respect to accountability policy. Such periods of issue drift, of course, have always occurred periodically in the peculiar way we make policy in this country. Reflecting on this condition, in a chapter revealingly entitled "On the Gravity of Americans and Why It Does Not Prevent Them From Doing Ill-Considered Things," Tocqueville puts it particularly well: "habitual inattention must be reckoned the great vice of the democratic spirit." The good news here is that shifting political attention and the dominance of bigger issues mean that in the next few years, we in higher education will frequently be left to our own devices. The bad news, in turn, is that when political forces *do* focus upon us, though seemingly at random, they will come on strong. More important, they will likely lead with assessment — either in the form of the "cross-cutting skills" and "good educational practices" foundations of the corporatist vision or in the "back-to-basics" admonitions of the New Right alternative.

Where does this leave us with respect to accountability? On the one hand, the imposition of systematic regulatory, quality-assurance approaches of the kind that we faced in the late eighties is unlikely, either in the form of big federal mandates or concerted state action. On the other, no new model of quality assurance *not* based on regulatory action has as yet emerged. Under these conditions, the temptation is strong to simply enjoy the resulting confusion — sitting, as Tocqueville put it, in the "ruins of the old building." But I believe that this would be dangerous for several reasons. First, in the near term, there are some very real accountability phenomena that we need to deal with on a state-by-state basis as they arise. In the long term, I believe it is imperative for us to take advantage of this period of policy uncertainty to remake our

own brand of quality assurance, substantially different from what we have done in the past.

THREE CURRENT POLICY APPROACHES

Regardless of national twists and turns, most institutions are currently being forced to deal with some very real and directive policy approaches. The first of these, "performance funding," was, only a few years ago, viewed as a somewhat-quaint policy anomaly — working tolerably in Tennessee, but not adopted anywhere else. Now, depending upon how the term is defined, some eight to ten states have some kind of performance-funding system in place, and another five or six are seriously considering implementing one. Testimony about the scale of this explosion of policy interest from a different direction comes from Sandra Ruppert's recent interviews with sitting state legislators nationwide: 44 percent of those interviewed believe that performance budgeting will be implemented in the near future in their own states. As many of you are aware, probably the most prominent current example of this approach is in South Carolina, where a law was enacted last year requiring *all* public support for higher education to be allocated to institutions on a performance basis by the year 2000.

Several reasons underlie this growing fascination. First, performance funding is simple and is therefore compelling to lawmakers in its own right. "Pay for performance" makes good business sense, and legislators are increasingly advocating "businesslike," market-driven replacements for what they see as cumbersome government-run programs. Moreover, because accountability measures are built directly into the budgetary mechanism itself, there is no need to think about accountability as a separate issue and to really deal with its complexity. More subtly, as the state share of support for public colleges and universities shrinks, government is even *more* inclined to behave like a paying customer. In a recent piece in the *Chronicle,* for instance, David Breneman pointedly commented on the largely self-proclaimed progression of public research universities from "state supported," through "state assisted," to "state located" status — noting that even though state shares amounted to less than 20 percent of general operating funds in some cases, institutions cannot live without support of this magnitude that comes in the form of an entirely discretionary subsidy. Indeed, many state officials are increasingly taking this shrinking share as a signal for government to get out of the business of general-purpose funding entirely. Performance budgeting mechanisms provide them with a concrete way of doing so — acknowledging explicitly that government will pay for only some of the things that higher education does, just like everybody else.

Behind these overall observations lie some very specific trends in performance funding's underlying mechanisms. One is continuing diversity, as no two states are enacting this approach to policy in exactly the same way. As Joe Burke's continuing Pew-supported study of the phenomenon on a national basis reveals, most performance-funding schemes continue to rest on the use of available data, with particularly heavy reliance on statistical performance measures developed earlier as pure accountability devices. Most are not organized around a discernable "theory" of desired higher education performance or about how better performance might be induced. Nevertheless, the results of Burke's project do suggest some clear trends in the types of data that are being used. First, "consumer-oriented" measures like student and alumni satisfaction, access to needed classes and to faculty time, availability of desired services and financial aid, and employment-related outcomes measures such as job-placement and licensure-passage rates are increasingly prominent. There is also growing interest in measures of "institutional good practices" like post-tenure review, local resource-reallocation and restructuring pro-

"**P**ay for performance" makes good business sense, and legislators are increasingly advocating "businesslike," market-driven replacements for what they see as cumbersome government-run programs.

• •

cesses, and student assessment. Both trends, it is interesting to note, are putting a good deal of strain on established performance-budgeting mechanisms because they involve things that are difficult to count. Consumer-satisfaction measures are generally survey-based, with consequent statistical instabilities due to both differential response rates and the vagaries of instrument design. "Good practices," in turn, rely on judgment calls instead of hard measures — raising inevitable questions about who will make such judgments and under what circumstances.

Challenges such as these are forcing conversations about new forms of performance funding that rely less heavily on formulaic approaches than the Tennessee prototype. One alternative being discussed in several states, for instance, is to continue to use hard statistical measures to allocate about 5 percent of available dollars on a formulaic basis, while using additional "softer" measures to make special grants to institutions or to ground occasional base-budget adjustments. Judgment-call measures, moreover, provide an interesting occasion to evolve some different approaches to peer review. Several states considering the use of such measures, for example, are talking about using panels of expert assessors to visit institutions to determine the degree to which they are engaged in "adequate" (and therefore fundable) "good practices." If adopted, the resulting mechanism would look much like the external reviews of mandated institutional assessment reporting conducted in the mid eighties in states such as Virginia and Colorado. Highly focused, government-sponsored peer-review mechanisms with explicit links to funding of this kind, of course, have already been widely

As a result, the "market" only really works to drive quality in the manner intended for a small slice of high-end institutions that are either national or regional in character — those that end up listed in *U.S. News* or *Money* magazine, for example.

● ●

implemented abroad, including, most prominently, the United Kingdom, Australia, Hong Kong, and the Netherlands.

In considering the future of any performance-funding approach, it is also well to reemphasize the dominant pattern of political instability. On the one hand, it is quite clear that the logic of performance funding as a general approach to policy has enormous and growing appeal for state legislators drawn from both the corporatist and New Right traditions. As a result, the initiation of such schemes is likely to be strongly and broadly advanced in the coming decade. On the other hand, the specific contents and forms of these initiatives may shift rapidly with the issues of the day and, more important, with who is in office. Such circumstances, ironically, will probably make it more and more difficult for states to actually *implement* complex performance-based budgeting with any degree of coherence and will render quite a few of them, as in South Carolina, entirely unworkable in their original form.

A second quality-assurance theme that has become more and more apparent in state policy circles is "consumer information." By way of introduction here, it is important to recognize from the outset the degree to which market forces are being proclaimed as the principal policy alternative to traditional regulation-based approaches. Within this rubric, the emerging orthodoxy is to rely on measured "quality" to steer consumer choice. Choice, in turn, is expected to indirectly drive institutional improvement in a process highly reminiscent of the school vouchers approach to K-12 policy that first emerged a decade ago. In order to work at all, of course, policy

approaches of this kind require clearly understandable and widely disseminated information about performance to guide consumer choice — a requirement that leads directly to calls, such as Governor Romer's, for a "*J. D. Powers Report* for higher education."

There are, of course, many important limits to this approach in actually inducing quality — apparent since even the earliest attempts to mandate consumer-information reporting, such as the Student Right-to-Know and Campus Security Act passed in 1990. Probably the most important of these limitations is the fact that most students don't actually have a choice about which college they attend. The vast majority are constrained by geographic location and by the existence of other commitments to only a few alternatives, consisting largely of nonresidential, nonselective public universities and public community colleges. As a result, the "market" only really works to drive quality in the manner intended for a small slice of high-end institutions that are either national or regional in character — those that end up listed in *U.S. News* or *Money* magazine, for example. Arguably, of course, these are precisely the kinds of institutions that least need an external stimulus to assure or improve their academic quality.

Despite its obvious flaws, this growing policy emphasis on market mechanisms has critical implications for the ways in which we gather and report information. One is the fact that the focus of reporting shifts markedly from what individual institutions do to how particular types of students fare. Particularly relevant here, moreover, is the fact that a clear majority of students now attend more than one postsecondary institution in pursuit of a baccalaureate degree. This condition has always posed a well-known challenge to campus assessment practitioners who attempt to estimate the impact of a general education curriculum that only a few of their graduating students have actually completed as designed. From a consumer-information standpoint, it increasingly shifts the unit of analysis for reporting on the experiences of specifically identifiable types of students — young, traditional, day-attending, degree-seeking, for instance — in achieving equally concrete outcomes such as numbers of courses completed, completion rates, job placement, and so on.

A second important implication is that government is not the only — nor even the most natural — supplier of consumer information. As a result, there is growing state interest in the use of third-party information brokers to either collect such information or report it out. A number of states, for instance, are considering contracting with locally recognized opinion-polling or market-research organizations to obtain information about student and alumni satisfaction, instead of asking institutions to collect and supply it. At least two state systems, moreover, have employed nationally recognized corporate consulting or accounting firms to produce and issue their accountability reports. Both alternatives are pursued, of course, because of the higher market credibility involved in employing "business-related" outsiders to discharge such functions. A central implication of widespread outsourcing of this kind, though, is to render government's role increasingly one of background consumer protection — discharged largely by establishing information standards and by providing definitional consistency among the different kinds of performance measures being used. In many ways, this growing trend constitutes the real force behind the National Postsecondary Educational Data Cooperative (NPEC) initiative launched last year by the National Center for Educational Statistics (NCES).

Whatever the specific mechanisms selected by states, the bottom line is that we can expect growing emphasis on consumer statistics as a centerpiece of quality assurance in the next few years. Equally likely is a concomitant expansion of emphasis on the use of nongovernmental data collection and reporting within a broader rubric of government-sponsored consumer protection. This forecast, of course, leaves open the question of exactly who such nongovernmental third parties might be. Up to now, we in higher education have done little but complain about the abuses of such players as *U.S. News* and *Money*, without recognizing fully the natural niche that they are filling in an emerging market-centered paradigm of quality assurance. A more reasonable question to ask is how we might construct our *own* mechanisms for fulfilling this increasingly salient function.

This question leads to the changing role of what has lately been the "dark horse" accountability alternative — our own traditional mechanisms of institutional accreditation. Certainly, there has been an unusual degree of innovation and experimentation in this realm during the past couple of years — a healthy sign, I think. Regional accreditors are recognizing more and more explicitly that established models of the accreditation process — based on relatively long cycles of review, the preparation of a formal self-study document, and a relatively unfocused multiday site visit by an ad hoc group of peers — don't really work very well any more to either assure quality or cause improvement. On the one hand, the exercise adds little value to many institutions — especially if these are large ones where the environment gives internal managers opportunities to use the process for internal leverage and where their attention is already diverted by often far more frequent and more high-stakes processes of professional accreditation. On the other hand, the results of accreditation currently have little to say to the public beyond the fact that the institution meets the basics. Moreover, with the reauthorization process for the Higher Education Act under way next year, regional accreditors are especially eager to show that they can effectively discharge accountability functions. Their failure to do so during the last round of congressional action in 1992, you may recall, almost resulted in their being written out of the law.

Prodded by all these forces, regional

accreditors have, in fact, been experimenting with new forms at unprecedented rates. Many of these experiments, moreover, reflect growing recognition of the fundamental difference between stimulating improvement and assuring quality. Most agencies, for instance, now have an optional "dual" review process that some institutions can engage in, with one component focused on meeting minimum standards and another that allows institutions to engage in a set of approved locally determined activities. SACS and WASC have probably been the most prominent in pioneering this approach. At the same time, all parties are giving greater prominence to data, with a particular focus on outcomes. WASC, for instance, is currently piloting an alternative review process with several University of California campuses (together with the University of Southern California) that requires each institution to prepare a "data portfolio" for demonstrating basic compliance with established standards. As in the SACS alternative process, institutions are then free to engage in planning-oriented, in-depth self-studies on topics of their own choosing. Not surprisingly, the kinds of indicators chosen for inclusion in such portfolios look a lot like state-level performance indicators.

In parallel, accreditors are showing growing interest in using standard data definitions — preferably those being evolved by NCES or proposed by the American Association of State Colleges and Universities's Joint Council on Accountability Reporting (JCAR) project — in all their work. Standard data of this kind can provide a much better foundation for external communication than simply leaving how to count up to each institution. Such data are also far more likely to have already been collected by somebody — thus cutting down on the work required to prepare for accreditation. This latter advantage is echoed in a third line of experimentation on the part of accreditors these days, which is also focused on portfolios. In this case, however, institutions are asked to assemble a range of extant documents and

exhibits and present them to a review team, with only minimal commentary, in lieu of a self-study. On the one hand, this is expected to cut down on the work involved in preparing for review. On the other, exhibits of this kind are often far more credible in demonstrating the presence of an institutional commitment or a process in place than a specially written narrative.

REMAKING PEER REVIEW

These "new looks" in accreditation appear promising for the eventual development of a meaningful academically owned, nongovernmental approach to quality assurance. But as yet they have neither the commonality nor the clout really needed for the academy to retake the initiative. For a final few minutes, therefore, I'd like to speculate a bit about what it would take to do so. More particularly, I want to advance three "simple" themes for the future development of effective institutional peer-review mechanisms. In any situation of large-scale change, of course, such admonitions must be followed with caution. As Edmund Burke again reminds us in his *Reflections on the Revolution in France,*

> it is with infinite caution that any man ought to venture upon pulling down an edifice which has answered to any tolerable degree for ages the common purposes of society, or building it up again without having models and patterns of approved utility before his eyes.

Consistent with this fitting advice, each proposition advanced is not just an "idea" but something for which we do indeed have "models and patterns of approved utility" — concrete alternatives that we can begin to experiment with right now.

As a first step, I believe we must concentrate our academic quality-assurance processes to a far greater extent on the *academic integrity of the degree.* We are moving rapidly into a world in which credentials are not only sought for their own sake but also have very specific and powerful meanings for external stakeholders. As some of you may be aware, certification processes for everything from Novell network technicians to financial planners are being established throughout many industries, together with an enormous and growing commercial testing and assessment infrastructure to support them. Such processes have, of course, long been standard for individual certification in the professions — most prominently in such fields as health, education, and legal practice. In the face of this, we in the academy have no clear mechanism for asserting what our own core credentials — the baccalaureate and associate degrees on which these specialized credentials must necessarily rest — really mean. Certainly, we are currently unable to do so as an industry. At a lower level, we can only rarely make claims about core content for a single institution — much less be able to demonstrate how a given college or university is consistently committed, organized, and aligned to achieve identified objectives once they are set. With a new wave of political types increasingly ready to dictate academic content, I believe that it is more and more dangerous for us not to have such a vision, together with a means of showing how we are measuring up to it.

Established mechanisms involving peer review, like institutional accreditation, could be improved a great deal by focusing far more explicitly on this question. It is, after all, the question that both government and the corporate world have repeatedly asked processes such as accreditation to answer. Rather than being simply a proposition, however, alternative "models and patterns" are already available and could be pushed a lot further. One, of course, is the emphasis on outcomes and assessment now being pursued by all regional accreditation agencies as an integral part of their processes. These requirements, though, tend to be treated largely as add-ons to existing standards, rather than being used as the principal focus for reengineering the process

As a first step, I believe we must concentrate our academic quality-assurance processes to a far greater extent on the academic integrity of the degree.

• •

as a whole. More interesting possibilities are suggested by some of the alternative accreditation associations that are beginning to spring up, structured around institutions of like type. The newly established American Academy of Liberal Education (AALE), which is currently building a review process focused explicitly on the meaning of a liberal arts credential, provides a case in point. Similar associations — focused on different institutional mission emphases (and therefore appropriate degree contents) — can easily be imagined.

A second imperative, I think, is to focus peer review on *only a few core processes* that are demonstrably *related* to achieving degrees with integrity. Looked at from this perspective, current institutional accreditation standards are far too comprehensive. Evolved in an era in which higher education institutions were largely private endeavors subject to no external oversight, their coverage now duplicates things that government agencies are already addressing in areas such as finance, governance, and myriad specific procedures (e.g., human subjects research policies, student complaint and refund policies, etc.). Duplication of this kind not only wastes effort but tends to dilute the peer-review process itself. As a result, the typical accreditation visit too often involves compiling a laundry list of diverse things for the institution to "fix," advanced with no real sense of academic priority and requiring no special academic expertise to identify. Core academic processes, in contrast, are things that *only* reviewers drawn from the academy can evaluate effectively. Among the most promising of these are the design and conduct of undergraduate, lower-division instruction — especially in that vast, uncharted territory we call "general education" — and in some key factors and processes (such as use of the "Seven Principles of

Good Practice in Undergraduate Education") that we know through decades of research are directly responsible for student success. Despite legitimate diversity among college and university missions, these areas are, in fact, common across all types of institutions and have right and wrong answers, as well.

Here again, I would argue, we already have "models and patterns of approved utility." Although frequently maligned by institutions, one is illustrated by the review practices of specialized accreditors. In most cases, both the standards employed by such bodies and the level of scrutiny of curricular content and delivery that they involve far exceed those applied at the institutional level. Moreover, given the oft-heard complaint that the results of such processes can unduly leverage institutional resource allocation toward the professions, an institutional process focused principally on undergraduate general education might provide a badly needed counterweight. More fitting examples of how such a process might work can be found abroad — illustrated particularly by the peer reviews conducted in the U.K. until recently by the Council on National Academic Awards (CNAA) or, less completely, those currently used for funds allocation by the Higher Education Funding Councils in England, Scotland, and Hong Kong. In all three cases, these processes combine thorough curriculum review with actual inspections of instruction through portfolios and peer visits.

This leads to the third and final imperative — to focus quality assurance on the integrity and adequacy of *each institution's own quality-assurance and improvement processes*. Admittedly, this admonition is broadly consistent with what regional accreditors are already beginning to do — sometimes, perhaps, with what must seem like a single-minded vengeance to many of you. But they are largely doing so as an add-on to existing comprehensive requirements. Alternatively, the review of such processes might be made the real centerpiece of accountability by devoting the lion's share

of attention to it in both established accreditation standards and in the actual conduct of peer visits. Two recent pieces have prominently argued for an "academic audit" of this kind — one by Graham, Lyman, and Trow, supported by the Mellon Foundation, and one by Dill, Massy, Williams, and Cook, appearing last fall in *Change* magazine. In many ways, this approach also resembles that used in the national Baldrige Award process — an alternative equally championed by many for application in higher education settings. Meritorious though these suggestions are, I would argue that they cannot ultimately be meaningful for quality assurance in the absence of the previous two foci — the integrity of the degree and the quality of core teaching and learning processes. The purpose of an audit of any organization, we must remember, is to be able to believe and interpret the bottom line that it reports, and it is with our own "bottom line" of outcomes and core teaching practices that I believe we must begin.

In many ways, of course, the sentiments behind all three injunctions have already been expressed many times by working groups within and outside the accrediting community. WASC's *Report on the Future of Self-Regulation in Higher Education* was among the most forward-looking of these, as were the many conversations and planning documents surrounding the now-defunct National Policy Board effort. I think, in short, that we already know what to do in many of these areas. And despite an uncertain (and occasionally alarming) political context, I think that it is imperative for us to make progress on some of them. Toward the end of *The Social Contract*, Rousseau writes in an appropriate vein that

every free act must be produced by the concurrence of two causes: the one moral, that is to say, the will must resolve upon the act, and the other physical, that is to say, the power that must execute it.

In a revealing reversal of Rousseau's "causes," I believe that we have already fulfilled the physical condition. Bumpy and uncertain though the environment may be, its very construction provides us with a rare opportunity to forge some new kinds of consensus. What remains to be seen is whether we are up to the moral task of "resolving our collective will" to make it happen. ◆

REFERENCES

American Association of State Colleges and Universities. *A Need Answered: Recommended Accountability Reporting Formats.* Washington, DC: AASCU, 1996.

Burke, Edmund. *Reflections on the Revolution in France.* Library of the Liberal Arts. New York: Bobbs-Merrill, 1955.

Burke, Joseph C. *Performance Funding Indicators: What Do They Say About Concerns, Values, and Models for State Baccalaureate Institutions?* Albany, NY: Rockefeller Institute of Government, 1997.

Dill, David W., William S. Massy, Peter R. Williams, and Charles M. Cook. "Accreditation and Academic Quality Assurance: Can We Get There From Here?" *Change* vol. 28, no. 5 (Sep./Oct. 1996): 16-24.

Education Commission of the States. *Making Quality Count in Undergraduate Education: A Report for the ECS Chairman's "Quality Counts" Agenda in Higher Education, Governor Roy Romer, Chairman.* Denver: ECS, 1995.

Ewell, Peter T., Jane V. Wellman, and Karen Paulson. *Refashioning Accountability: Toward a "Coordinated" System of Quality Assurance for Higher Education.* Denver: ECS, 1997.

Graham, Patricia A., Richard W. Lyman, and Martin Trow. *Accountability of Colleges and Universities: An Essay.* New York: Columbia University Press, 1995.

Hobbes, Thomas. *Leviathan.* Parts I and II. Library of the Liberal Arts. New York: Bobbs-Merrill, 1958.

Rousseau, Jean Jacques. *The Social Contract.* Trans. Charles Frankel. Hafner Library Classics. New York: Hafner, 1947.

Ruppert, Sandra S. *The Politics of Remedy: State Legislative Views on Higher Education.* Washington, DC: NEA, 1996.

de Tocqueville, Alexis. *Democracy in America.* Trans. George Lawrence. New York: Doubleday/Anchor, 1969.

Western Association of Schools and Colleges. *Report on the Future of Self-Regulation in Higher Education.* Oakland: WASC, 1993.

Peter T. Ewell is senior associate at the National Center for Higher Education Management Systems, PO Drawer P, Boulder, CO 80302.

Though is the first AAHE conference at which I have played an official role, as incoming president, and I must say, there couldn't have been a better way to ease into the job. As those of you from Virginia know, I'm an old hand at assessment speeches. As the chief academic officer and coordinator of the assessment

Looking for Results
The Second Decade

BY MARGARET A. MILLER

movement in Virginia, for a decade I gave biannual speeches to the Virginia Assessment Group, and I have many times been a contributor to this conference. So I feel like I'm talking to a group of colleagues with whom I've worked for a long time, about an enterprise in which we all have a serious stake.

Because I've been watching assessment practitioners and making assessment policy almost since the inception of the campus-based assessment movement, I'd like to talk today about that history as I have seen it culminating in the four strands of this conference. I'd also like to speculate about the future of assessment. You're all probably tired of water metaphors to describe the environment we live in — whitewater, waves breaking, and so on — but they *are* compelling because of

the ways in which existing educational structures seem to be melting and flowing into new shapes and configurations. And assessment will play a major role in that reconfiguration, I'm convinced, if its practitioners can rethink and reshape their enterprise as well.

Let me begin my summary of what's happened at this conference by reminding you of what all four strands have in common: They all emphasize how assessment has led to action based on evidence about what students learn. I'm probably not the only person in this room who remembers what a cultural shift it represented for the academy to systematically track its effect on students — to create a "culture of evidence" and do something with that evidence. The next phase of assessment — during a time in which we're seeing a shift in

In our attempt to focus on discrete sets of skills, we risk losing the gains we've made in viewing education as a process eventuating in the total development of learners.

• •

attention from teaching to learning and from seat time to demonstrated mastery — would be impossible if it weren't for a decade of our taking results seriously and developing subtle and complex, not to mention valid and reliable, ways to measure them. But a certain historical irony emerges here.

As you will remember, the idea of assessing student performance in the aggregate was initially met with resistance, even outrage, by many faculty. That outrage, I came to believe, was due to the fact that we had shifted the locus of responsibility for educational success from the individual student to programs, which means to the faculty and its curriculum and pedagogies. But in the subsequent decade the academy has become increasingly destabilized. As research by OERI and others has demonstrated, students at most institutions are taking longer to complete their degrees, and they may stop in and out many times during the process, as well as move from institution to institution. For those students, a burgeoning majority, whatever coherence traditional curricula and programs had is disintegrating, and no one set of people is responsible for what they receive in the way of intellectual fodder. The Western Governors University represents an extreme version of this trend: Responding to the needs of peripatetic students, it will not have recognizable programs, faculty, or facilities, but merely credit learning when it sees it. This forces assessors to focus once again on the individual student.

The challenge this poses is in how to ensure that when we award degrees to those "mall" students, as Cliff Adelman calls them, we do so on the basis of cumulative development rather than isolated fragments of learning. In our attempt to focus on discrete sets of skills, we risk losing the gains we've made in viewing

education as a process eventuating in the total development of learners. I would suggest that the only way we can solve this difficult problem is for consortia of institutions to do serious assessment of the learning gains of the students who swirl among them.

The four strands of the conference reflect the two original motivations for assessment: improvement and accountability, the two parallel lines about whose eventual meeting we were initially so naively hopeful. Classroom and out-of-class assessment both reflect the movement's driving concern to improve learning. The accreditation and institutional effectiveness strands have stressed their role in institutional improvement, but the activities described in this group of sessions also demonstrate to higher education's external constituencies that it is engaged in quality-control efforts and is accountable in that sense. Performance measures, as we have seen, go even further in giving those constituencies information about outputs or outcomes as indicators of institutional effectiveness — sometimes with, to use Peter Ewell's term, "brutal" results.

Classroom assessment is the purest form of assessment-for-improvement, because the information gleaned can immediately be used to improve teaching and learning. The brilliant contribution of classroom assessment to the movement is that its focus on immediate feedback is both good pedagogy, as Grant Wiggins so eloquently explained, and makes possible curricular adjustments where students most directly experience them. There have been many heartening examples at this conference of completing the loop between assessment and improvement at the level of the program or university. But in general, the further away from the individual classroom you get, the harder it becomes to turn assessment data into useable information. Reasonably enough, faculty's sense of their responsibility and power to effect change is proportional to their sense of ownership and control over the educational experience, which is strong in the classroom and gets progressively weaker through the program and general education levels, and — with some happy exceptions — typically exists not at all for out-of-class experiences. But as a character in one of Toni Cade Bambara's short stories put it, most people don't just want a side order of this and a side order of that — they want the blue plate special. As I said in talking about focusing on the individual student, I think we have to continue to try to meet the challenge of assessing student learning and development as a whole, even when we distribute responsibility for the various parts of it. In this case, that entails cooperation not among institutions but between those two nations within a single institution, student affairs and academic affairs.

Again, some history: When I came to the State Council of Higher Education for Virginia, the first job I was assigned was to develop guidelines for assessment in the state. Nowhere in them was there mention of the extracurricular aspect of college life and its effect on student development. Then we started listening to students, and we discovered that classroom learning was one of the four or five most important things that happens to them during college. I should have known this, of course — about a third of my own education at UCLA happened in the classroom; a third in my dorm room; and a third, during my junior year abroad, mostly in French cafes. The University of Virginia's longitudinal study demonstrated that students today have a similar experience and that, moreover, this is intentional: Of the ten goals the UVA students had set for themselves while in college, only four were clearly classroom-related. They are rediscovering the legacy of Mr. Jefferson, who, with Lee Knefelkamp, believed that the academic village should cultivate not only the knowing head but the honest heart. The Germans would lump the development of both under the term *Bildung*.

So I was impressed by the number of pre-sentations during this conference that focused on attempts by academic and student affairs staff to combine their tools for a more complex assessment strategy designed to capture student development in its totality. I think it signals another of the breakdowns of academic structures to which I alluded at the beginning of this speech: The Berlin Wall between the curriculum and the extracurriculum is, I think, beginning to come down. Some of the most powerful learning strategies we have are focused on *Bildung* rather than narrowly concentrated on cognitive development: service-learning or internships, for instance. Increasingly, we are trying to create learning communities in which deep learning can occur, which seems not to be a matter simply of cognition but to involve the entire character. We need both a sophisticated understanding of what characterizes such deep learning, as Ted Marchese has pointed out and as other sessions have reinforced, and a multiplicity of tools with which to assess it, in order to promote it.

And we need to tease out the differences between the kinds of deep learning likely to occur in traditional undergraduates and the learning that the new majority student — that is, a middle-aged woman pursuing a master's degree part-time — needs and wants. How do we foster that student's development outside the classroom?

I said that the University of Virginia students were unknowingly circling back to Mr. Jefferson's founding idea of the honest heart as a goal of education, and the accreditation strand of the conference gave me the sensation of circling back myself — in this case, to the first assessment conference in Virginia, ten years ago, which was jointly sponsored by the Council and the Southern Association of Colleges and Schools. SACS was, I believe, the first regional accreditor to develop an institutional effectiveness criterion. Since SACS's approach to outcomes assessment was completely compatible with the state's, Virginia's public institutions have done very well on that criterion. Perhaps that's why I believe that the accreditation community's initial commitment to assessment has been successful.

But times have changed for accreditors. As academic structures break down, the processes on which they have historically focused their attention are in some cases disappearing. The advent of cybercolleges presents the most radical challenge: If they are refused accreditation because they have few of the features on which the review has historically focused, higher education can be viewed as protectionist. Just after I wrote those words, interestingly enough, an article in the June 16 issue of *Forbes* made just that claim. Such "protectionism" is particularly problematic, the authors point out, at a time when even traditional institutions are beginning to deliver education through some of the same means. The inevitable consequence of the move to new delivery modes, it seems to me, is that accreditation's focus on outcomes measures to ensure quality will intensify dramatically.

And accreditation faces yet another challenge. In the tension between improvement and accountability that has plagued assessment since its inception, accrediting agencies have stressed the improvement agenda, as the sessions in this strand of this conference make clear. But accreditation also performs an accountability function, in that the process of accreditation was meant to ensure that higher education had quality controls in place, though the results were confidential. But the public seems less and less convinced that those controls are working, as evidenced by the recent state-level push for performance measures and effectiveness indicators. I agree with Peter Ewell and Edward O'Neil, the latter of whom said in a recent *AAHE Bulletin* article that accreditors are best situated to develop measures of effectiveness that are acceptable to the public's representatives and that institutions agree are the grounds on which their effectiveness should be judged. But I don't think this can be just a matter of accreditors

helping each institution develop an individual set of measures that will make it look good, as O'Neil seems to imply when he encourages accreditors to "coach institutional customers in best responses." I think accreditors can honor the diversity of institutions by asking them to find measures that reflect their individual missions, while at the same time the accreditation community develops a core set of measures across institutions and regions. And the results, I would argue, should be made public, clustered in peer groups to discourage inappropriate comparisons. To do so may even contribute to the improvement agenda: Consider Grant Wiggins's point that performance is enhanced by deprivatizing assessment. But it is certainly necessary to the accountability one. Peter Ewell is, as usual, right — someone (institutions, the federal government, state agencies, accreditors, or *U.S. News & World Report*) will tell the story of higher education's performance. I hope that the academy will seize the opportunity to speak for itself candidly, accurately, and, above all, comprehensibly.

Having worked on indicators of institutional mission and performance measures in Virginia, I don't underestimate the difficulties of finding core measures that are central, valid, robust, comprehensible to the public, and so on. More broadly, committed as I am to the improvement agenda, I am very well aware of the difficulties of protecting it in an era of accountability. I just don't think it's a challenge we can fail to accept. The alternative, a set of performance measures developed by a budget office, is not, I can assure you, a pretty sight.

The final strand of this conference, institutional effectiveness, addresses what is fast becoming *the* issue in higher education: How can we organize ourselves to be more effective and productive enablers of learning? We are being asked by every public constituency from the U.S. Congress on down to do that job more cost-effectively, and we will be crushed between the Scylla of competition and the

Charybdis of regulation if we don't attend to that need. In order to do so, we will need to bring a number of things into better alignment: an understanding of what learning is, the needs of our students, our learning goals for them, our teaching practices and delivery modes, the learning environment (including out-of-class experiences), assessment, planning, budgeting, and public communication (including both talking and listening to our constituents). Most of these issues have been addressed separately at this conference; in some sessions the interrelationships have been addressed. I consider this alignment the biggest challenge that now faces the higher education community, and AAHE will be focusing increasingly on helping colleges and universities meet that challenge.

Years ago, in Virginia, the Council said that no project would be eligible to receive money from the Funds for Excellence program (which was our competitive grant program) unless it was justified by assessment results. I remember that Clara Lovett, now president of Northern Arizona University but then the provost at George Mason University, said that that stipulation didn't work at all, since assessment was about the past and the grants were about the future. It is true that assessment measures what has happened in the past, but as should be clear from what I've said already, I believe that it is most decidedly about the future. I think assessment will become, and in some institutions has already become, an indispensable rudder as we chart a course through strange and dangerous seas filled with "Here Be Dragons!" signs. In order to do that, though, assessment must not be a compliance exercise or a train on its own track, to borrow an old cautionary phrase from Peter Ewell. Assessment needs to be in the thick of things, acting rather than reacting, and doing the following jobs:

It needs to work in partnership with psychologists, neurobiologists, learning specialists, and faculty to refine our understanding of learning and to track its traces in students.

We are being asked by every public constituency from the U.S. Congress on down to do that job more cost-effectively, and we will be crushed between the Scylla of competition and the Charybdis of regulation if we don't attend to that need.

● ●

It needs to bring that understanding to bear on powerful learning strategies: active learning, reflective practice, learning in groups, just-in-time learning, multisensory learning. Through assessment we should be able to discover how to combine those strategies — through service-learning, undergraduate research, case studies, cyberlearning, internships, co-ops, and so on — to generate the most learning as efficiently as possible and to use faculty time as effectively as possible.

Assessment also has a responsibility to address public concerns and answer public questions. One of the issues that's on the public agenda right now, as Lee Knefelkamp pointed out in the keynote address, is affirmative action. When the gates of the academy began to swing open after World War II, and particularly after the 1960s, the higher education community began increasingly to assert as a fact that a diversified student population promotes learning for all students. On my more cynical days, I think of this as an opportunistic argument, designed to justify the growing enrollments that drove increased budgets; on others, I think that most members of the academy have a deeply held commitment to access. In any case, this was not an intuitively obvious point to previous generations, despite Henry Adams's assertion that he learned nothing from the other Bostonians at Harvard but only from the Virginians, and it is not intuitively obvious to affirmative action opponents today. But when we have been challenged on the benefits of diversity, we generally have simply said, "No, you don't understand — we all agree that it's really, *really* a fact that diversity benefits students!" It's time for more of us to seriously address as a

But at some point, I think we need to develop, as a community, some rough consensus about what the degree actually certifies.

● ●

research question the issue of the learning that occurs among students and the effect of differences on that learning and to make those results widely known. I do understand that capturing the effects that students from varying backgrounds have on one another — beyond the ability to mouth what we consider correct opinions — is like catching moonlight in a net. But a community that has the brainpower to measure complex molecular structures surely has in it researchers who can do this job as well.

This connects to another public concern, the one about standards. Several sessions at this conference have addressed the issue of standards, specifically the alignment of high academic standards in high school, graduation requirements, and admissions standards. Our public communications about admissions — that is, what selective institutions tend to brag about — focus on test scores, which means that it should be no surprise to us when those scores are taken as the sole measure of an incoming student's worthiness and preparation for and capacity to do college-level work. We need to support the good work that is being done to develop better measures of student readiness for college, such as performance assessments in high school, and track the subsequent success of students whom we admit on grounds other than high test scores. We also have an obligation to determine which kinds of support we give those students actually work in helping them to succeed — and then, of course, to do these things.

And I suggest that we be prepared for our own graduation standards to come under scrutiny. What are we saying, when we award the baccalaureate degree, about the student's ability to think, solve problems, and communicate, for instance? To some degree the marketplace judges, however crudely, the effec-

tiveness of individual institutions at producing employable graduates. But at some point, I think we need to develop, as a community, some rough consensus about what the degree actually certifies.

That consensus will, I hope, reflect a rich notion of what college does for students. In talking about the meaning of the degree, we need to determine how the skills, knowledge, attitudes, and values we purport to foster would actually manifest themselves in post-graduation life. For example, recently I worked with the assessment coordinators in Virginia to develop some common questions that they all would put on their alumni surveys. Virtually every institution says that it prepares students for citizenship, or what Lee Knefelkamp calls "democratic intelligence," but when it came to the questions we might ask about that, we were stumped. Should we ask them if they vote? If they volunteer? If they are active in civic organizations? What did we want to see? Moreover, one of the reasons we say we value diversity in our student populations is that we want students to have skills that they are willing to use to benefit the entire community: black, white; poor, rich; urban, rural. But do we actually ask our graduates about that and correlate those results with the characteristics of our entering classes? In short, what are our criteria for success beyond subsequent satisfaction with education received, salary, and employer satisfaction — which are undoubtedly important but limited measures? If we aren't sure, you can bet that we didn't make it clear to students.

Finally, let me conclude with the opportunities presented to assessment by the new teaching technologies. I've already mentioned the challenge to accreditation presented by the cybercolleges, which is how to accredit an educational institution that may have no programs, for instance. But here are some other issues that technology will force:

First, the technologies force the issue of assessment itself: Because of the massive investment they require, the demand for demonstrable results is imperative. On the other hand, they facilitate assessment, since authentic student production is stored in a convenient nonlocation, cyberspace.

Learning is not a job that pays by the hour. We already know this — most of us wouldn't be willing to jump out of a plane wearing the parachute of a parachute packer who came to class every day and barely passed the course, even though he or she had the right number of credits to be certified. But all technologies force the issue. Take the book, for instance. American faculty, when asked about the trade-offs between cyberlearning and class time, sometimes say that students really need to be in class a certain number of hours per week (say, one per credit) in order to learn. But they have already allowed the technology of printing to displace a good deal of contact time. In Hungary, for instance, where books are hard to come by, students routinely spend three times as many hours in class as American students do. So how many contact hours equal the credit for one semester? The twelve to fifteen hours per week that American students spend or the forty to forty-five hours that Hungarian students do? And if time spent in class isn't the basis for credit, then what will our new currency be?

We do *need* a currency — that is, credits. Narrative descriptions of student learning have the drawback of a barter system. A standardized currency creates portability, which is critical with as mobile a student population as ours. In systems without credits, students can't transfer between programs inside the same institution — never mind going elsewhere to continue their education. But if credits aren't based on contact hours, what will they be based on? Can the assessment community help develop a learning-based currency that will be less devalued than the one we have now? If it can do so, it will have rendered higher education an enormous service.

The contact-hour issue raises yet another important question about face-to-face instruc-

tion: To what degree is physical proximity a necessary condition of deep learning? Socrates certainly worried about the issue: He considered the development of literacy detrimental to learning, primarily because books are noninteractive. Telepresence, email, and computer-aided instruction make the new technologies superior in that respect, of course: One of the most interesting findings about the effectiveness of telecommunicated instruction, in fact, is the sense students have of increased interaction with their professors in online courses. But even in using a non-interactive technology like the book, obviously we have decided as a literate society that not all learning needs to be proximate. What we haven't determined are the amount and nature of the interactions, and with whom those interactions need to take place, in order to change students. This will probably vary by age, gender, and ethnicity, which complicates the picture. Even further complicating it is our interest not just in cognitive development but in *Bildung*.

And there may be kinds of growth that are possible with the new technologies but that are hard to accomplish in the traditional classroom. The Flashlight Project, for instance, has discovered that using technology in teaching results in improved abilities of students to apply their knowledge, work in groups, and continue learning on their own. It makes it hard to design control-group experiments when the outcomes may be fundamentally different in the two kinds of experience.

All of this is daunting but also very exciting. Assessment, in its tenth year, is just now hitting its stride. But its forward momentum depends on you. I predict that given their present disarray, some of the external forces that originally drove it, such as state agencies, will apply occasionally intense, but intermittent, pressure over the next few years, and it will be easy to relax your efforts during the lulls. But apart from self-interest, I suggest that you not flag for intellectual reasons. You could spend the rest of your professional lives answering some of the most fundamental and exciting questions there are about human development and the ways to foster it, and in the process shaping higher education's future in important ways. I, for one, want to be a part of that process.

So let me tell you how AAHE intends to be in on the conversation. Our plan now is that next March, the National Conference on Higher Education will be focused on learning, with three strands: the new brain research and what it and other disciplinary explorations of learning tell us about deep learning; teaching strategies that we know from experience to be powerful; and the ways in which institutions should organize to focus on learning. I hope you will join me in Atlanta March 21-24, so that we can learn from one another about these issues. ◆

Margaret A. Miller is president of the American Association for Higher Education, One Dupont Circle, Suite 360, Washington, DC 20036-1110, aahepres@ aahe.org. Before coming to AAHE in July 1997, she was chief academic officer of the State Council of Higher Education for Virginia (SCHEV).

I now know that I have two things in common with Michael Jordan. First, like Michael, I was cut as a sophomore trying out for the varsity team (soccer, in my case). Second, as you might guess from my voice, is that I'm getting over the flu. When I consider the effort it took to get on an airplane to be with you today, I'm staggered at Jordon's

Feedback
How Learning Occurs

BY GRANT WIGGINS

performance in the NBA finals, playing with the flu and leading his team to victory.

His performance is actually a good lead-in to our topic: feedback — a word we use a lot, a word front and center to why we're all at this conference. But feedback is a word that I've learned over the years really needs some analysis, some careful thought. Unthinkingly, people often misuse the word. So I want to talk very basically about what feedback is and isn't.

To get back to Michael Jordan and athletics: One obvious thing in watching good athletes, and even in listening to them in interviews, is that they often make clear just how vital ongoing feedback is to their mastery. I was particularly struck by Tiger Woods's recent remarks when he won the Masters'. When asked how

he turned around his early poor performance, he described how, on the back nine, when he was not playing well, he said to himself that he had to adjust his performance. But to know you need to adjust, you need ongoing feedback. Tiger knew he needed to adjust on the basis of the feedback that he was receiving — not from any person, psychometrician, or indirect proxy test but from the real thing, the unintended effects of his putts and his drives.

So I want us to think today about a point that is utterly commonsensical in the wider performance world, but still hard to grasp, oddly enough, in schools (where one would think that exemplary learning takes place): You don't get good at anything without feedback — not feedback in the sense that an expert translates things for you, but feedback

We in the academy still cling to the view that learning is a straightforward, linear affair: We teach, students learn, and tests reveal what and whether they learned.

●●●●●●●●●●●●●●●●●●●●●●●●●●●●●●●●

in the sense of watching the ball, where it goes and where it doesn't go, and realizing what the result means for your next actions. To show that feedback enters into all learning and self-adjustment, consider some simple examples: We use feedback as we drive by looking at road signs to making sure we're heading in the right direction; or we use feedback from a videotape that tells us what we did and did not do on our swing — or in your classroom.

Lest the references to driving or sports strike you as a tad unintellectual in a forum such as this, let me refer to Plato and to the Socrates whom we find in Plato's dialogues. The very idea of a dialogue immediately alerts us that feedback and reaction will be central. Indeed, what makes the dialogues not only so interesting and charming but also so powerful is that Socrates invariably takes his cue from the words and ideas of his co-participants. He doesn't have a canned speech to offer. Indeed, if you compare two dialogues — say, for instance, the "Meno" and the "Theaetetus" — they begin very similarly but progress differently as a result of the reactions of the two namesakes. Each is puzzled by Socrates's request for a single conception (virtue and knowledge, respectively) after each has listed examples. "I want to know what the examples have in common," says Socrates. "Try again." And then the dialogues diverge in tone and depth because Meno fails to grasp the nature of the request and Theaetetus immediately sees the error in his first response. One might say that the rest of each dialogue takes shape around the feedback that Socrates receives to all of his questions and to all of his answers.

So let me say it again, commonsensically: If you want to accomplish a purpose, you need feedback. So, today, let us suspend fancy talk of validity and reliability. I simply want to talk about that part of assessment that concerns

judging whether the performer is accomplishing goals and about the role of feedback in both learning and assessing.

But common sense ends at traditional testing. Our initial axiom that all accomplishments require feedback, when applied to student performance during and after assessment, begins to look quite radical. Ironically and sadly enough, though the rest of the world seems to understand the importance of feedback in how it conducts its affairs, we in the academy still cling to the view that learning is a straightforward, linear affair: We teach, students learn, and tests reveal what and whether they learned. Further, it seems as if teaching itself does not need feedback. Many syllabi are impervious to feedback (namely, diverse student responses, interests, or trouble), so much so that some professors reuse syllabi year after year: If it's the first week in November, it must be supply and demand or *Paradise Lost*. When there is formal feedback from students, it is requested and given at the end of the course — when it can do little good (especially in terms of giving the students a sense that the professor is listening).

Consider the wider world by contrast. This is the era of consumerism, and we are better for it. On my flight here, when it was time to land and I had to put my computer away, I picked up the airline's magazine from the pocket in front of me. The little insert that I have here in my hand says: "At Continental, we're listening. We care about what you think, so give us a call any hour, any day. At Continental, we won't just lend you an ear. We'll pay for the call. We want to know what you think about flying with us. What are things you like? Is there anything you'd like us to change? Whatever your thoughts, we want to hear them. So give us a call, fax us, or simply fill out the response card and send it in."

I'm one of those silly people who actually replies. I have called an airline or hotel or car rental, sometimes just to tell them that things are okay. (They like that because they're not used to those kinds of phone calls.) But, invariably, I'm treated with respect, even when I have a bitter complaint. I'm treated with reasonable sympathy, if not empathy. All well and good, all common and familiar to those of you who travel and fly in airplanes or stay in hotels.

And yet, and yet . . . when was the last time your college or university really made a vigorous push to find out not only what student clients thought and believed and felt but what institutional clients believe and feel about your former students — not as a side effort by your alumni office but as a major initiative by deans and provosts?

I am reminded of an unusual such event that happened in the Louisville, Kentucky, school system when the Gheens Academy was responsible for professional development and reform a decade ago. Influenced by the total quality management (TQM) movement and a desire to really prove to the citizens of Louisville that the schools were more responsive, school officials did something extraordinary. Jefferson County Schools is about the thirtieth-largest school district in America, with more than a hundred thousand students. Between September 1st and October 1st in that year, the school system called every single family in the district, every single one. And they began the phone call by asking, "How are we doing?" Well, this was unheard of — think about when and why parents get calls from school about their kids. It generated an outpouring not only of good information but of goodwill that was hard to beat.

Feedback is neither a luxury nor ancillary to performance. A recent article in the *New Yorker* talked about the history of the development of HDTV, high-definition television. It was developed by a curious process, not the usual sort of mythic way in which people with good ideas and a think tank have light bulbs flashing, get a great idea, and run with it as entrepreneurs. No, on the contrary, said the author of the article. The ultimate product was developed by feedback, based on many conversations between the government and the television companies. The article said, in closing, that this is now the way of the world. Recent studies have shown that most modern, computer-related innovations, 70 to 80 percent of the refinements and the major features, are proposed by customers through feedback. Indeed, the downside of this, and all of you who live and die with software know it, is that it's become common practice to release beta software for sale to get feedback from people about where the bugs are in order to make the software better.

Some might even say that the result of polling and focus groups, the coin of the realm of modern politicians, is the realization in the late twentieth century that we don't really understand all of what we need to do until we hear what many different people think. Now, some people have blamed Clinton and Gingrich and other politicians for having no spine, no will, no vision, no leadership. I say, by contrast, "Hallelujah!": This all sounds like democracy to me. Find out what people think. (Which is not to condone pandering in place of wise judgment; let's err on the side of responsiveness for a change.)

Why is it, however, that we don't gather feedback regularly in schools and colleges and use it to improve service, to improve teaching? That's a puzzle to me. Let's think about it a little further. I'd like to make four simple points about this puzzle:

(1) You can't learn without feedback.

The next three follow from this first point, which I've already made, but they apparently are not self-evident to many educators.

(2) It's not teaching that causes learning. It's the attempts by the learner to perform that cause learning, dependent upon the quality of the feedback and opportunities to use it.

(3) A single test of anything is, therefore, an incomplete assessment. We need to know

whether the student can use the feedback from the results.

(4) We're wasting our time inventing increasingly arcane psychometric solutions to the problem of accountability. Accountability is a function of feedback that's useful to the learner, not to a handful of people who design the measures. The more arcane the measure, the less likely it is that it will cause any useful progress, despite its validity and reliability. Or to say it the other way around, the more self-evident the feedback to the performer, the more likely the gains.

Let's think about these points a little bit further by clarifying what I mean by *feedback*. If I did a poll about your definition of *feedback*, you would probably say something like, "Feedback involves telling someone what you did and did not like or what you did or did not judge to be right in what they did — some praise and some blame." If you ask people about their bad feedback experiences, they usually say things like, "Oh, I really got hammered by the person." The implication is that, in this profession, we still think that feedback is what you get from people who do or do not like something you did. That, of course, is a mistaken view. Feedback is not about praise or blame, approval or disapproval. That's what evaluation is — placing value. Feedback is value-neutral. It describes what you did and did not do.

When I was traveling through Boston the other day, I read in the *Boston Globe* about my beloved but depressing Red Sox. The article contained an explanation from the pitching coach about why the Red Sox's chief relief pitcher, Mr. Slocum, had been recently banished to the bullpen. It seems the pitching coach saw, in looking at videotape, "that Heathcliff did not find his location spot 22 out of 29 times. And when that happens, you know that he's not striding properly. And when that happens, you look at his delivery and, sure enough, we saw that he was striding in such a way that he planted his foot four, five, six inches to the left of where he normally plants it, throwing the ball consistently outside." Notice that there is not one negative or positive value judgment in that account by the coach, merely a description of what the videotape revealed. That's what feedback is. No praise. No blame. It just describes what you did and did not do in terms of your goal.

The best scoring rubrics for student performance do the same thing. In fact, when we work with people on the design of rubrics, we always say, "The rubrics will be powerful and useful to the extent that you rid them of value and comparative language, such as *excellent, good, fair, poor, better than, worse than, clearer than,* and *less clear than.* Substitute for all that phraseology discrete descriptors of what is actually true of a certain level." So, indeed, we do understand the importance of description in terms of rubric design.

I have a nice example from my son when he was four. Writing his name, he said, "Look!" When I saw what he was doing, I put on my Piaget hat. (Don't be alarmed; they're on to me now. You don't have to call the child-abuse people.) I said, "Gee, Justin, that's really interesting. What does it say?" He replied, "It's my name." I said, "Show me." He did: J-u-s-t-i-n, Justin. But his N really was ambiguous: It could have been an H. So I asked, "What's that last letter?" He said, "N." After writing a block N and a block H, I asked him to identify each, and he did. Then I asked, pointing to the letter that he'd written, "What's that?" Now here's the most important part of this whole speech — forget everything else, but remember this — with a long pause and the congenital Wiggins furrowed brow, my son's precious words were "Not what I wanted!"

Notice that he didn't say, "I'm sorry you didn't like it" or "Not what you wanted." He said, "Not what I wanted!" And that's the way real feedback works. I have an intent, I cause an effect, I discover to my dismay it was not the effect I intended, and I work very hard to honor it differently. I own this problem. When it's real feedback, I own it. I'm not angry at the person who gave it. People are hungry for real feedback that helps. When someone takes the time to carefully look at and describe what they have done, from their vantage point, that's a good feedback system.

Let's bump it up from children to college. Some of you know about two significant findings in the work of Dick Light and the Harvard Assessment Seminar. The chief finding from the Harvard Assessment Seminar about the most effective courses at Harvard, as judged by students and alums, was the importance of quick and detailed feedback. Students overwhelmingly reported that the single most important ingredient for making a course effective is getting rapid response. Students suggested it should be possible in many courses to get immediate feedback. A second major finding is that an overwhelming majority of students were convinced that their best learning takes place when they have a chance to submit an early version, get detailed feedback and criticism, and then hand in a final revised version. Many students observed that their most memorable learning came from courses where such opportunities were routine policy.

When I was in the education department at Brown, working with Ted Sizer, I taught one course per semester. In one of the courses that I taught, I did something that I had always done as a high school teacher, which was to make the first paper assignment and the last paper assignment of the course the same assignment. I had Brown juniors, seniors, and MATs tell me that this assignment was one of the most significant events in their years at Brown, in terms of helping them understand what they had and had not known initially, how much they had and had not made progress on the ideas of the course.

What my anecdotes, the Harvard example, and my experience suggest is, in fact, radical in the commonsensical. It's the idea that assessment is not an episode in which a test is taken, it's over, and results are given. An assessment

Students overwhelmingly reported that the single most important ingredient for making a course effective is getting rapid response.

● ●

must include the student's ability to use the feedback, because that's what eventual autonomous performance requires.

We've heard a lot during the past ten or fifteen years in both the higher education and K-12 settings about the importance of student self-assessment. Despite the importance of the idea, it is a misleading phrase. Self-assessment is not the goal. Self-adjustment is the goal. That's what makes Tiger Woods and Michael Jordan great. That's what makes Socrates so impressive. That's what our best students and teachers do. They self-adjust, with minimal effort and optimal effect.

All well and good. But suppose students have never been taught the importance of self-adjustment. Indeed, how are they ever going to be taught it in a scope- and sequence-coverage curriculum with a one-shot test? Regrettably, we still live in an assessment framework inherited from the Middle Ages, one predicated on a defunct theory of learning. That theory of learning says: "Take it all in, contemplate it, play with it a little bit, give it back, and we'll then certify that you understand. And if you don't understand, well, you can't enter the guild, the medieval tradition of the university."

The modern view, however, says: "No, that's not how it works. It's more like software. It's like basketball. It's like learning to print your name. You don't really understand it unless you can adjust. Unless you can cope with feedback. Unless you can innovate with what you learn."

Two examples from professional academic practices are illustrative. A simple example happens at this kind of forum. How many times has it happened to you? You hear somebody give a really interesting talk, and then when the question-and-answer period comes, the person embarrasses him- or herself. You

What is considered intelligent, adaptive, and responsive behavior by performers in every other venue is considered cheating in schools and colleges.

● ●

conclude that the speaker does not really understand the subject. Or consider the pinnacle performance in formal education. Why do we have the dissertation and also its defense? We have the defense because the dissertation is insufficient. Four hundred pages and eight hundred footnotes are necessary but not sufficient evidence of understanding. As suggested above, understanding is often only revealed through dialogue in the broadest sense: dialogue with people or dialogue with experience and phenomena. Assessment must reflect this fact.

Some very innovative practices in places abroad do this now. One of my favorites is in Great Britain, in science K-12. A number of performance tasks designed for the national assessment ask the student to design simple scientific experiments. For instance, one of them involves watching and playing with a wind-up toy. The question then asked is, "What's the relationship of wind-ups to linear distance?" — appropriate because the toy goes all over and is not very predictable. The student has to design a little experiment to answer the question. After an hour or so, the student writes up his or her results. Then the assessor asks, "Great, now that you know what you know, how would you redesign the experiment, in light of the results, in light of the question, and in light of the scientific method?" Evaluators found an interesting thing. They found that almost half of the students who had perfectly reasonable answers nonetheless could not justify their methods or propose deficiencies in their method.

We are only slowly learning to grapple with the phenomenon of student misconception, that wonderful but disturbing research that began in physics twenty years ago at Johns Hopkins (and is now noted everywhere, in part thanks to Howard Gardner's wonderful

book *The Unschooled Mind,* in which he summarizes all this research). In the absence of interactive assessment, in the absence of assessment that doesn't require students to use feedback and respond to it, student misunderstandings can be hidden behind their correct answers. In the British practice, the British experimenters actually gave as many points to the answer to the question as to the original experimental design, and here's the sad footnote. The National Assessment of Educational Progress (NAEP) borrowed the British task and six others and used them in its hands-on science assessment seven or eight years ago. But it took out the latter part of the test. It didn't score students on their response to questions. It only asked the students to design the experiment.

Let me give you a different example. The Province of Quebec has begun to practice what I'm preaching as a system. The sixth- and tenth-grade writing assessment for students is multiday, and the students bring previously written and evaluated work to the exam. They have to revise previously written and graded papers. They seek feedback during the exam. That's called "cheating" in most places. And that shows you how far we are from understanding this commonsensical message. What is considered intelligent, adaptive, and responsive behavior by performers in every other venue is considered cheating in schools and colleges.

Someone who had this down to a science was an eleventh-grade English teacher in rural Ohio. He said to his students:

> I want you to do peer editing, and I want you to do two things, and two things only. I'm going to teach you how to do it because too much peer editing is the blind leading the blind, pooled ignorance. Here's what you're going to do: (1) Attach to your draft a statement of purpose. 'What was I trying to do in this paper?' The peer editors will respond in terms of that pur-

pose. Not, 'Ah, I liked this, I didn't like that,' and the other kind of random things that sometimes are helpful and sometimes not in peer review. But, 'Okay, you were trying to do this, but here's how it seemed to me.' (2) Mark the place on the paper where you lost interest and explain why.

I've told this English teacher story a lot of times during the past few years, and the amazing part is the number of teachers and professors who are disturbed by this idea. They actually find it difficult to imagine that they might confront students with the fact that their writing is uninteresting or boring in places. And yet, what's the most common thing you hear about student papers anywhere in the world? That they're boring.

This teacher finishes off the "lesson" in just the right way. Ultimately, feedback is for empowering the performer. He doesn't set up the peer reviewers as God. On the contrary, when students submit the final draft, they must tell him which feedback they took and why, which feedback they didn't take and why, and then attach a final self-assessment to their final paper. That's a teacher who understands today's message. That's a teacher who gets extraordinary results from not particularly gifted students. That's a teacher who understands not only that we should not shy away from feedback but also that it is essential to how we get good at things.

Dick Light, in the Harvard Assessment Seminar report, went on to describe the parallelism for professors of what he had asked students: "Faculty members at Harvard were asked what single change most improved their teaching. Two ideas swamped all others. One is enhancing student awareness of the big picture, the big point of it all. The second is the importance of helpful and regular feedback from students, so a professor can make midcourse corrections."

Probably everybody in this room works at an institution where some form of final course evaluation is normal or even, perhaps, policy. But final course evaluation makes the same mistake as final testing. It's at the end, when it's too late — too late in a very important sense. You might say, well, it's not too late. The professor is going to teach the course again. No, it's too late for the students. The students don't have the satisfaction and the moral respect of seeing their feedback make a difference. Or worse, they see that it doesn't.

I had a colleague, when I taught, who asked the same two questions every Friday. He handed out index cards on which students answered the questions "What worked for you this week?" and "What didn't?" Notice the language. Not: "What did you like?" Rather: "What worked?" He always was surprised. And he's a good teacher. What worked for Joe did not work for Jill. I get feedback to almost everything that I do now in writing, either on scan sheets or in written comments, and I'm always stunned at the enormous disparity among some of the comments. Some people think I'm the greatest thing since sliced bread. Other people think I should be run out of town on a rail. Some people think I'm sensitive to the problems, the issues, the audience. Other people think I'm arrogant and aloof. What the hell do I make of it? But that's the challenge! That's teaching. That's performance. That's customer relations. That's assessment.

Interestingly, a high school student who used to work for me went off to Harvard this year as a freshman. I asked him to collect for me examples of Harvard exams. (Harvard is unusual in that it places all freshman exams on reserve in the Freshman Library. In fact, exams have changed enormously over the years. Exams from 1901 are all "Trivial Pursuit." If you think we haven't made gains, go look at some of those early exams.) Our friend found two exams that he said he knew I'd be interested in, and I was. The professors gave the students 20 or 15 percent credit for a full appraisal of the course's strengths and weaknesses in terms of the criteria that the professors laid out, and for student recommendations on how to improve the things that they thought were deficient. Yes, it's done at the end. But giving it exam credit sends a message.

As I suggested a few minutes ago in the British story, and as many of the other examples from the wider world indicate, the next great leap in assessment is to understand that a solitary test, in which there is no interaction between the person taking the test and the assessor, will turn out to be as foolish, dimwitted, and premodern as some of the practices involving rods and canes were a hundred years ago. If we want to know if students understand something, we have to see if they can deal with feedback and with counter-arguments to their arguments and their own ideas, just as we do in the dissertation's defense.

But as the stories also illustrate, it's not necessarily a function of human one-on-one. Feedback built into assessment is about compelling the student to have her or his ideas intersect with reality, to see if the balsa bridge will hold the weight predicted by the physics the student proposes using — to see if the student can convince the client that this solution to the problem of environmental pollution is, in fact, feasible scientifically, economically, and politically. Indeed, one of the most exciting things to me about the so-called problem-based learning in the professional schools — in medical school, business, engineering, and the like — that's now finding its way into the collegiate and precollegiate world is that problem-based learning, by its very nature, builds feedback and the need to use it into the work. Even if we are only able to simulate it, we can nonetheless alert students that they have to show that they can deal with feedback. They have to show that they can deal with the unexpected to be said to truly understand and be skilled.

Indeed, if we take this lesson to heart, we will come to a very disturbing truth that follows from the commonsensical premise that we began with. None of us who has been a teacher is anywhere near as good as we can be, if we are not routinely getting feedback from students. It's as if Michael Jordan had to wait until some psychometrician gave him the score from the game a week later. It's as if the player can't see the ball go in. It's as if the person speaking to his audience can't tell if he's boring them and putting them to sleep. If all we get back is a psychometrically derived, indirect score, if all we get back is what we put into our students, we can be sure that they're not getting all of what they could get and give. We can be sure that there's so much to understand about what they don't understand.

In this regard, one of the most striking things about the Harvard Assessment Seminar reports is that professors relate that the single most useful addition to their teaching repertoire, and the way to hone the two points earlier identified as most helpful in improving teaching, is the so-called "One-Minute Essay" (where old friend of AAHE Pat Cross is cited as the originator). At the end of each lecture, professors ask, "What were the most important points today?" and " With what questions do you leave?" What a shock it was to some professors to discover that what was so clear, elegant, thorough, concise, and self-evident made absolutely no sense to all those eager-beaver Harvard undergrads. That is the point of feedback.

So I leave you then with a plea. Instead of resisting regular feedback, embrace it. In terms of your own assessing, stop confusing feedback with praise and blame and give far more genuine feedback, or contrive situations that force the student to seek and respond to situational feedback. Praise is necessary. (Blame is sometimes also necessary.) But praise only keeps you in the game. It doesn't get you better. Feedback gets you better. And the student is entitled to more of it than the student normally gets.

In closing, as a cautionary reminder, I note the story I told six or seven years ago in this forum, for those of you who were here. Mike comes up to his tenth-grade teacher at the end of the year and says, "I really like your teaching, but you kept writing this word all over my papers, and I don't know what it is." "What was the word?" she asks. "*Vagoo*" is the reply. As a former English teacher who wrote the word *vague* many times, on many papers, I didn't find the incident as funny as the audience. It was, in fact, painful. And that, of course, is the point. What seems like self-evident feedback from our point of view isn't necessarily so to the learner. And therein lies the pathos of teaching.

Now, some would say that when students become undergraduates or graduate students, it's their problem. Let them figure out what's wrong with their work. Such responses show me that we're not there yet; we're not yet understanding how learning and assessment work. They show me that Continental Airlines still has much to teach us on this subject. We need the feedback of (even) the novice to achieve expertise.

So I leave you, then, with this idea. Feedback is not praise or blame. It's what you did and did not do, whether you realized it or intended it. Assessment should make its chief business the confronting of performers with the effect of their work, including performers called teachers. And then performers must do something about the effect, either to explain it, to justify it, or to correct it.

I await your feedback. Thank you. ◆

Grant Wiggins is the president of The Center on Learning, Assessment, and School Structure (CLASS), 648 The Great Road, Princeton, NJ 08540-2516.

I'm here to talk about listening to the people you serve — the impact of quality improvement on effectiveness. I'm going to start with a story that may not seem related to that topic, but I'll explain later. Sometimes it takes the exceptional to reveal the routine.

When the phone rang at 4:30 on Saturday

Listening to the People You Serve

BY ELLEN EARLE CHAFFEE

morning, April 19, I was sound asleep in Mayville, a town of about 2,400 with a university enrolling about 750 students, located about 40 miles from Grand Forks. It took awhile to realize that this was no dream. The chancellor was calling from the state emergency center in Bismarck.

"We're losing Grand Forks," he said. "How many can you take?"

"How many what? What for?"

"Before this is over, all 50,000 residents will probably be evacuated. They're starting with one small area now, but it could go fast. How many can you take?"

Neither of us knew what we needed to know in order to answer that question. What do people do when they're ordered out of their homes? Where do they go? How long

would they stay? What would they need? This seat-of-the-pants decision making was to characterize at least a dozen decisions we made every day for two weeks.

Past blizzards had taught me that food stocks for the weekend would be the critical factor. I woke the new Marriott food service director and then called the chancellor back.

"Two hundred if they need meals all weekend, 400 if they're passing through," I told him.

He went away for a few minutes and came back on the line.

"I told them 1,000," he said. "They're desperate. Do whatever is necessary to help these people. And keep a log with their names and addresses."

Those were the only instructions I ever had

We had no one with disaster relief experience. It was all but impossible to get sound information from anyone anywhere.

● ●

and the sum total of my training as a relief center director. I called the three vice presidents and the director of the physical plant, who had been sandbagging his own home in Fargo, fifty miles away. I grabbed what seemed potentially useful (all the pads of paper and pens I could find, a roll of masking tape, and a box of tissues) and headed for the student center. By 6:30 that morning, the Mayville State University Relief Center was open for business.

The MSU Relief Center registered nearly 2,500 new friends. We doubled the community's population in the first four days. Up to 300 lived on campus and up to 2,000 more in homes in our service area. Only about thirty people spent as many as three nights on cots in the field house, so the standard concept of a "shelter" did not apply to us. At first, most guests lived in a residence hall that had been partially converted to house the education faculty. Those faculty and others took turns staffing the building 24 hours a day to provide hospitality and a listening ear for our troubled and anxious guests. We served 1,000 free meals a day, with never a peep from Marriott about who would be paying for it. In fact, Marriott staff from colleges in three states donated their days off to come and help our staff.

Some of our new friends were state legislators and University of North Dakota faculty and staff. Many were blue-collar workers and retirees. One group was from Bosnia. A few guests were homeless, mentally ill, or were, as they say, "known to the police." Most arrived with no pajamas, some with no shoes, and some with their shoes and pants still wet because they wouldn't stop sandbagging until the National Guard dragged them out. They ranged from infants to frail elderly, and they brought their dogs, cats, fish, and birds.

By the end of that first day, Saturday, we had free on-campus and community-based housing, a computerized registration system, free 24-hour food service, registration for people staying locally and those passing through, pets in dorms, pet care at the local zoo, a phone bank, a volunteer scheduling system, a volunteer-hours documentation system, 24-hour emergency medical technician presence, and access to electronic mail for our Grand Forks guests.

In addition, by the end of Sunday, we had a big-screen TV with a continuous display of information for guests, a TV tuned to Grand Forks news coverage, message boards, a donation of $354 from a special offering at Aurdal Lutheran Church, a supply of emergency cash to give out no questions asked, an ecumenical church service on campus, a list of all registered guests posted for guest review and search, an informational site on the World Wide Web, free child care, and toys, games, and books for children.

By Monday, we had free swimming, open access to the library, a daily newspaper called the *High Ground News,* and live music at every dinner and most lunches. We had a full array of social services, and more than a dozen informational programs on topics of interest to our guests. Makeshift stores in six locations gave away all the clothing, personal supplies, food, bedding, and other goods a person could want (except that the most popular item, new underwear, was slow to arrive) — an estimated $1 million in donated goods that we unloaded, sorted, and distributed from semis and U-Hauls arriving daily from Wisconsin, Illinois, Montana, and elsewhere. In true higher education fashion, we soon had a system of self-governance, too, operated by a group we called the Friends Committee.

Together, we watched the core of the Grand Forks downtown business district burn to a crisp and their city water supply turn to sewage. Together, we figured out how to deal with reporters from NBC, CBS, ABC, MSNBC, *People,* the "Today Show," Fargo,

Minneapolis, and the *Des Moines Register.* Together, we learned about FEMA, SBA, flood insurance, and angel money.

Our comprehensive services continued for nearly three weeks, and we housed and fed people for seven weeks. We did all this with absolutely no assistance from the Red Cross, which was overwhelmed with other sites, and occasional food deliveries from the Salvation Army. Faculty, staff, and community members registered enough volunteer hours during the first two weeks to equal more than 1,100 eight-hour shifts, not counting Marriott staff time. At least half a dozen people worked 16-hour days for sixteen days in a row. Local people gave more than $40,000 for emergency cash — more than $150 for every man, woman, and child in the community.

We had no one with disaster relief experience. It was all but impossible to get sound information from anyone anywhere. At one point, high officials from two different disaster agencies told me, within the space of an hour, that the thousands of people on cots with no running water at the Air Force base "definitely would" and "certainly would not" soon be evacuated to other shelters. We had no way to plan ahead — the situation changed hourly.

Relief Center jobs were created on the spot as our new friends taught us what they needed and were held by whoever was willing to do them. Volunteers did custodial work during the midnight-to-four shift, because the physical plant staff couldn't keep up with all the traffic and new duties. Several nights, those volunteers included three Ph.D.'s (two division chairs and a vice president), a business professor, and the director of the university's foundation. One night, the foundation director noticed a Grand Forks friend watching him sweep. She said, "I do that for a living up at UND — I'm just checking out your technique." He promptly offered to accept her guidance on how to do it better.

Some of the key overall leaders who emerged were the vice president for student affairs, the director of the career center, and an education professor. But I could name at least a dozen more key leaders, some who were working in their areas of expertise but most who were not. We established a sense of community among our guests by encouraging them to volunteer, too, when they felt able. Helping one another became contagious. Very quickly, a sense of teamwork and shared pride began to develop, in which each of us would have been our own worst critic if we had let anyone down, teammates or guests.

I claim no personal credit whatsoever. All I did was make five phone calls at the start and then hang out trying to be useful. I have no idea where all the volunteers came from. Every time a guest asked me a question I couldn't answer, I found that someone had posted a notice or set up a help desk to deal with it. I gave only one bit of guidance to our personnel — treat them like students.

In short, we knocked ourselves out. We cried with shared pain, and we cried from exhaustion. We laughed. We laughed a lot. We hugged. A lot. We amazed one another. We amazed ourselves. A lot of people needed us, and they needed us a lot. Geez, it felt good! My standard reply to compliments was, "It is a privilege to be in a position to make a difference in people's lives at a time like this."

Our new friends were very satisfied customers. It often seemed that they were more concerned about thanking us than they were about their own chaotic personal situations. Several notes emphasized appreciation that they were treated always with dignity and respect. Our new friends signed a huge thank-you banner, and many have offered their support for any future legislative battles. As one UND professor was leaving after four days, he handed us a donation of $500. A Grand Forks legislator sent $250 to be used not for our new friends but for those who had helped them. One couple told me that a volunteer EMT spent four days searching for their elderly neighbor and friend who had been undergoing chemotherapy, finally finding him alone among thousands at the Grand Forks Air Force Base and arranging for his transport to a regional hospital. A little girl's sad comment about a lost doll had led to her family's unofficial adoption by a local family, complete with a daughter her own age and an abundance of dolls, toys, clothes, and playmates. The grateful daughter of a guest organized $100,000 worth of donated goods to be delivered from Rockford, Illinois. These were the most satisfied customers I have ever seen.

To make all this possible, we canceled the remainder of the semester, fifteen class and exam days, and sent our students home. Overnight, we had a new mission. We became a home away from home, a full-service port in the storm. Or, as our FEMA friends came to call us affectionately, "the country club shelter of them all."

We had not the slightest idea who would pay the $4,500 daily food bill. We refunded $35,000 to students in room and board fees, even though our bond reserves are chronically short and we still have no way to cover it. It was not until the fifth day that I realized how vulnerable we were to a lawsuit if one of the guests we had placed in a local home ran off with the silver. We were running up overtime costs like mad in the physical plant, just eight weeks shy of the end of the biennium, the magic day on which our skinny little budget must show "break even" or be in violation of the state constitution. I told all faculty and staff that they would be paid their normal salaries for working at the Relief Center. For more than a week, I was sure that I would be called to task by someone, someday, for diverting the resources of the state without legislative authorization. I still consider it a real possibility. As the extent of noncovered costs becomes clear, people will be looking for someone to blame.

Knowing this, a visiting disaster official was stunned by our going out on so many limbs, to the point that he asserted more than once, "Very, very few people would do what you are doing." And yet my favorite quote, appearing in *U.S. News & World Report,* put his amazement in perspective. A reporter asked a nearby resident why she had opened her home to strangers, no questions asked. Her reply: "You're not from around here, are you?"

Depending on your criteria for evaluation, this could be a heartwarming story of doing the right thing or the worst business decision a president ever made. But from the perspective of listening to the people you serve, quality improvement, and institutional effectiveness, it is instructive.

I attribute the Relief Center's success to three primary factors: the university's decades-old tradition of providing personal service to students, the culture of quality improvement that we have been developing, and although this may surprise you, the farm background of many area residents. The personal-service tradition is genuine and bone-deep. The farm background provides us with folks who notice what needs doing now, who think about what else is needed, and who take the initiative to do it.

The center's focus was customer service, and the staff listened to the customers with all five senses and a brain. By that I mean that as often as our flood friends said something like, "Where can I get some underwear?" they told us their needs without words. No one said to me, "Where can I get a sense of security?" — but it was written all over their faces. And our job at any given moment was to serve whoever was in front of us. We had no habits and routines we could use without thinking about them. We had skills, we had tools, and we had resources. But effectively putting them into action required a sense of purpose. There was no debate about the mission of the Relief Center, no mistaking that our purpose was to meet the needs of these people. It was more than a purpose — it was a calling. Believe me, when the crying baby before you has no diapers or the truck driver asks you where to unload the food . . . you have a calling!

In addition, we all had the freedom to serve. By that I mean that we were not restricted by old habits, job descriptions, or bureaucracies. This is often called "empowerment." I don't like that word because it implies that power belongs to someone and can be granted to another. The word that I prefer is "liberation." Each person was free to choose, free to do. The center was evidence that, given freedom of choice, people will do the right thing.

I told you at the start that my story might seem not to relate directly to the topic at hand. Let me try to tie the two together, then move on to implications for colleges and universities.

First, I must confess that I just plain wanted to tell you this story. It has been a powerful experience in many lives, my own included. Disaster victims need to talk about it, and I guess disaster helpers do, too. Beyond that, though, the story holds profound lessons regarding many important issues and relationships, including our topic this morning.

I suggest that flood friends and students are not all that different, that being a relief center calls for many of the same behaviors as being a college, and that the principles of quality improvement are equally valuable in both settings. We and our colleagues do not have careers in higher education because of the pay, the power, or the prestige. We want to serve. Ultimately, even the most dedicated researcher is driven by service to others. Ultimately, even the most authoritarian administrator is usually motivated by the desire to ensure quality and service.

When we see a friend in a new place or in different clothes, we notice things we've never noticed before. In its relief center role, I noticed something about Mayville State, something related to service. I used to think that Mayville State's service orientation was an important fringe benefit. I'd rather have it than not, but it was frosting on the cake. I've changed my mind. Now I see the service orientation as the wellspring for everything worth doing — but only if we define service as doing that which the other person wants and needs. Doing nice things because we feel like

Depending on your criteria for evaluation, this could be a heartwarming story of doing the right thing or the worst business decision a president ever made.

● ●

it doesn't count. My service view is now sharply focused enough that I begin to see some discrepancies in how universities typically conduct themselves. We want to serve, we think we *are* serving, but in some ways we miss the mark. To fix those discrepancies, we need to make some changes. Our alphabet needs fewer I's and more U's.

Service is a core idea in quality improvement. Some of the key elements of quality improvement as understood through a management philosophy once known as total quality management (TQM) or continuous quality improvement (CQI) are:

● customer service
● develop human resources
● commitment
● process improvement
● measurement
● data-driven

My own experience with CQI is this: First, it embodies everything I know and believe in from reading, research, and experience about what constitutes good management. Second, it's a lot easier to read and write about than it is to do. And third, much more energy is wasted debating its value than is expended making serious efforts to apply it.

Going back to the service idea, customer focus — listening to the people you serve, meeting your customers' needs — is key in CQI. We in higher education are ambivalent about making a full-scale commitment to customer focus. Some believe we know better than our customers. Maybe so, to some extent, but there's more to the story, and that's what I want to play out here.

For the balance of our time, I'd like to describe the systems that produce too much silence in the people we serve, show the impact of that by using mission statements as an illustration, and describe how we might

One must conclude that we in higher education have a very forgiving environment in which we do not detect and may not correct many of our lapses in service.

• •

take a different view of many other key ideas if service were really the wellspring of all we do.

Compared with other kinds of enterprise, universities and colleges are systematically deprived of input from the people we serve. A consumer who buys a car or a house can be expected to say something if there's a problem or an opportunity to improve. Our students invest that much money, and two to four years of time out of their lives as well, but we may be less likely to hear from them for a variety of reasons. These include the fact that many of them are not paying the full price personally — their families and governments subsidize them. Our younger students may value their time investment less than they would if they had full-time work experience or hungry families. Problems they have with our services are often intangible, arise over a long period of time, or may be invisible to our students because they have no basis of comparison or the ability to form sophisticated expectations of us.

In addition, a baccalaureate student may deal with forty or more faculty members as service providers over the years, making it difficult to pinpoint responsibility for problems, and the student's complaints have the potential to work against him or her through the grading system. An enterprise that cared deeply about the people it serves would mount an extensive system to gather feedback under all of these handicapping conditions. Instead, we typically have a relatively weak system, with end-of-term surveys, if that — too late to improve a course while the student is still enrolled in it. And too much of what we call "assessment" is aimed at judging the student without informing the educational process.

Add to these factors the likelihood that students have little capacity to make a well-

informed decision about which school to attend and what to study, that they have little opportunity to try out colleges or courses, to shop around, or to return unsatisfactory credits, and one must conclude that we in higher education have a very forgiving environment in which we do not detect and may not correct many of our lapses in service. It is even difficult for us to hear from our alumni or their employers, unless we make special efforts to do so. Such an environment helps us stay in business by concealing our problems, but it does not help us achieve maximum effectiveness.

The primary point is that the very structures in which we work inhibit our ability to hear from, let alone listen and respond to, the people we serve. It is understandable, then, if our patterns of thought and practice are not, as they say in business, as "customer-driven" as they may need to be. Understandable? Yes. Tolerable in the long term? I think not. But rather than make that case, let me point out how I think this problem has affected our mission statements.

The mission states what we are trying to achieve. To get there, we chart a path through our strategic plans. Strategic plans represent an ideal path — in daily life, we make the improvements as best we can, and we assess the situation from time to time to see whether the changes are leading to the desired results.

This is really the simplest possible picture of my topic today: the impact of quality improvement on institutional or unit effectiveness. Of course, quality improvement impacts effectiveness. It's true by definition.

But too often it doesn't work out that way. Not all changes are improvements. Not all assessments lead to change. Not all results are as intended.

I think we'd do better if we simplified our terms to focus our attention. Our mission defines the results we seek; our strategic plans and improvements are the changes we'll make to better achieve those results. I suggest that any leader who wishes to improve institutional effectiveness keep these two ideas at the forefront of his or her thinking all the time. Think less about the mission statement and more about the results we're after. And talk more about results. We are obsessed with process in higher education. We need to become equally obsessed with results. Think less about the strategic plan and more about the changes we need to make in order to achieve the results. Certainly, the Relief Center couldn't afford to be casual about results — the only process we had time for was the one that got the necessary results.

There's another key word in the quality philosophy, one that I won't be discussing today: *trust*. We would be fully effective if we spent all day, every day, focusing only on our best efforts to earn trust and to offer trust to others. In the context of a focus on results and change, trust brings to the table the idea that the results and the changes will be worthwhile and that folks won't be hurt in the process. But that's another speech.

Let's say that you are going back to college. You are considering two institutions, and you decide to check out their mission statements. How many of you know the mission statement of your own institution? It's long, right? So you probably don't have it completely memorized. But bring it to mind as best you can. I'm going to ask you to compare it with the ones I'll give here. Now, as a potential student, you decide you want to go to the college that aims to get the results you want, and you think it's fair to expect the mission statement to tell you the results the college is trying to achieve. Here is example #1:

X State College is a public, comprehensive, land-grant institution serving [the state] and the nation.... Its mission is the provision of instruction, research, extension, and other public service programs for all segments of the population to achieve their ... goals.
Here's #2:
The mission of X College is to improve the lives and personal success of our students, associates, and the larger community by providing superior learning opportunities in the arts, sciences, and professions.

How many of you would go to institution #1? How about #2?

Which is more like the mission statement of your own institution? How many of you have a mission statement that's similar to #1? To #2? I've read *a lot* of mission statements. My guess is that at least 75 percent of them are more like the first example.

What's the difference between the two mission statements?

The first statement focuses on what the people at the college do. The inference is that if you think that's neat stuff, we'll let you come along with us. Let me make a radical proposition: The purpose of your university is not to provide you, as an employee, with the opportunity to do what you want and get paid for it. But you'd never know it from most mission statements.

The purpose of your university is to help people. You help them prepare for careers and for satisfying lives. Your research and service help people solve problems. The only difference between theoretical and applied work is how long it may take before it helps people. Put another way, if what we're doing doesn't help people now or later, what justification do we have for using their money and their time? I think we really do want to help people, and in the main, we succeed. Why don't we say so? Why don't we focus on doing it better? I think it has to do with the systemic silencing of the people we serve. And I think one consequence of that is that nobody knows the mission except when we're arguing about changing it. The mission doesn't say what's in our hearts, and so, like the strategic plan, it gathers dust on the shelf.

If we really understood our mission to be helping people, if we thought about how to do that better, we might begin to see and do things differently and, in some cases, to do different things.

Here are some transformations I think we need to make that arise from taking a service-driven point of view. These are just a few of the possibilities, but they illustrate the shifts we could make. The topics I've chosen are *mission,* which we've already talked about, *instruction, core competency, distance education, technology, goals,* and *assessment.* The great news is that some of these transformations are already becoming quite evident in our literature and practice, and I hope they will flourish.

For example, this change of perspective is becoming an increasingly familiar topic of discussion. Our faculty teach, but their purpose is to help people learn. The shift in focus from teaching to learning may prove to be the most powerful force for change in this and the coming century. I hope so. I think its impact is only beginning to be felt. When most faculty members are driven consciously by the desire to help people learn, I predict we'll see changes in how they relate to students, grading, homework, scheduling, the use of class time, and the definition of cheating, for example. For an excellent discussion of these and related issues, be sure to read Alan Guskin's "Restructuring to Enhance Student Learning (and Reduce Cost)" in the Spring 1997 issue of *Liberal Education,* published by the Association of American Colleges & Universities.)

The strategy literature in business emphasizes knowing what the organization's core competence is. At the core of the organization, what is it that you do best? Knowing the answer puts the organization in a position to expand its services by expressing its core competence in new ways. For example, the Swiss used to think their core competence was making analog watches. They learned, too late for some companies, that their core competency was something else, like helping people tell time or performing precision workmanship at the highest level of quality.

We tend to think that our own core competencies are teaching, research, and service. Again, though, this definition is based in what we do, rather than the benefits we offer others. The core competence of Harvard might be . . . hmmm . . . I'm tempted to say "fund raising." But taking a benefits perspective,

Harvard might say "discovering and sharing new and advanced knowledge." The variation I like for my small colleges and many others like them is "instilling competence and confidence." If we think of ourselves as being in the competence and confidence business, it puts a fresh spin on the role of athletics, gives us a new view of our potential role in the age of welfare reform, and has important implications for how we select new faculty and what kinds of professional development opportunities we offer.

If we understand that our mission is to help people, and if we know that many people want to learn but cannot come to us, then we have a different view of distance education. It's in the same family as workforce training, lifelong learning, and every other category of service to those with time and place considerations that don't fit our traditional-age straightjackets — which, by the way, don't fit people of traditional age very well, either.

And yet, we persist too often in trying to make educating people at a distance as much like traditional education as possible. Has research documented the necessity of a 50-minute class period for effective learning? Does the effectiveness of the lecture method justify its frequency of use? Do people learn better in the daylight hours and on weekdays? Do they all start with the same level of prealgebra knowledge and learn algebra at the same pace? If we are really listening to the people we serve, we will be working on how to customize education for each individual learner, not how to push lecture-discussions out to as many people, in as many places, as possible.

And let me ask you this: How many of you can name five faculty colleagues who could lead a panel discussion on what research has shown to be the most effective teaching strategies and the conditions under which they work best? How many of you can name five for a panel discussion on learning styles? It strikes me as one of the great ironies of our research-based enterprise that so few of us are really experts on the research that informs —

or should inform — our primary activity.

And the same goes for all the incredible technologies at our command. Online discussions among instructional technology people include debates about how to assess the effectiveness of computer-enhanced learning. My campuses, for example, issue notebook computers to all faculty and students. My board wants to know whether doing so improves student learning. I can tell you right now, the answer is, "No. Notebook computers do not enhance learning." It's not the computers; it's what faculty and students do with the computers that may enhance learning. Technology is not an end; it is a means — and in that respect, it is no different from lectures, field trips, or lab experiments. Remember to focus on the results you want. If you want students to develop computer skills, then give them computers. But if the desired result is to improve student learning in academic areas, don't expect that just giving them computers will do the job.

Think back to the two different mission statements — one focusing on what we do, the other on the benefits to the people we serve. If we focus on what we do, our technology vision might be "whoever has the most toys wins." The more toys we have, the more we can do. This is a popular model. A recent Yahoo! survey ranked colleges on the basis of criteria such as how many computers they had, the availability of server space for student home pages, and the number of network connections ("a port for every pillow" was the ideal). At first, my major gripe was that Yahoo! only surveyed about 10 percent of the institutions in the nation. But the more I think about it, the more persuaded I am that the survey missed the point entirely. It's not how many toys you have. It's not even how much you use them. The question is, do your faculty know and use the teaching strategies and tools, including technologies, that best foster effective learning? Our mission is to help people. Technology is just another input.

In the first mission model, we do things, we

If we are really listening to the people we serve, we will be working on how to customize education for each individual learner, not how to push lecture-discussions out to as many people, in as many places, as possible.

• •

think we're good at it, and we want to be recognized for it. Maybe that's why so many universities seem not only to enjoy but to actively seek a listing in the many top 10, 20, or 100 lists that so many popular magazines are producing. I'd enjoy it, too, and I'd market it like mad. But we're not managing toward their indicators, and we're certainly not manipulating our numbers for a better slot.

We produce an annual report to investors, showing trends in our performance on the key indicators our constituents want to know about. I prepared for the first edition by researching the indicators used in national rankings — maybe we could kill two birds with one stone by informing our constituents and raising our national rankings at the same time. It didn't work. We're not managing toward the magazines' indicators because so few of their indicators have anything directly to do with our constituents' definitions of quality or service. To pursue a high ranking is to put something else above helping people — namely, our own prestige.

We could identify many indicators of how well we help people, and those would make better goals. One that I like is 100-percent retention. Properly defined, that would mean that we attract the right people and do the right things with and for them. Another might be high student satisfaction ratings or ratings by employers of our graduates. Frankly, and here comes another radical statement, I don't give a rip what *U.S. News* thinks of my university. I want to know what Mark Friestad thinks. And Marijo Vik. And the superintendent of schools at Casselton.

And when I find out what they think, I don't take it as the last word, even if it's a rave review. I've got news for you and your least-favorite governing board member (the one who wants to know whether you're better than the college down the road) — there is *no* last word in this game. In fact, this is not a game, or at least it is not a competition with a final score. Harvard will never be better than Stanford . . . nor the reverse. Most of the people I deal with couldn't care less about Harvard or Stanford. The difficulty that so many of us have in treating assessment information as input to our improvement plans is in part, I think, an indication of just how over-committed we are to the concepts of competition and winning. Our commitment needs to be to the person before us right now, and the ones we'll see in the future.

This student won't get another chance to learn Biology 101 the first time. Colleges and universities are taking dollars from each student's pocket and time from each student's life, and the students won't get either the time or the money back again. It should be a crime to make the same stupid mistake as last semester; we should consider it immoral to throw away information that could help us do better the next time. And I use those strong words advisedly. We are no less culpable than a general contractor or a manufacturer. In fact, I'd say we have a far greater obligation. We are taking time from people's lives, promising that to do so will make their lives better in the future. They can pay no higher price; we can do no less than maximize their learning for a lifetime.

In conclusion, the primary lesson of the Relief Center for me, and the primary theme of these remarks, is the need to listen and respond to the people we serve. We've been doing that to some extent. There are ways to do it wrong, and we must avoid those. But there is still too much "I" in our approach.

If only we learned to put "YOU" at the center of it all, if only we learned to make results more important than activities, then we would remember our mission. It would feel more like a calling. We would knock ourselves out,

amaze ourselves, and amaze each other. Our results would be more powerful, and our changes would be more effective.

I want to thank AAHE for giving me this opportunity to say what's on my mind. Now, I hope you'll say what's on yours. It's my turn to listen to the people I've been trying to serve. Thank you very much for your kind attention. ◆

Ellen Earle Chaffee is president of Mayville State University and Valley City State University, 101 College Street South, Valley City, ND 58072.

Assessment, accreditation, improvement: These are three terms well known to the higher education community, and all are capable of provoking responses ranging from religious fervor to extreme distaste to complete cynicism. Rarely are they mentioned together. Ask a group of educators to define any or all of

Intentional Improvement

The Deliberate Linkage of Assessment and Accreditation

BY SHERRIL B. GELMON

these terms, and one will get a range of interpretations. Yet the activities represented by these three terms — assessment, accreditation, improvement — are increasingly assuming more prominent roles in higher education at a time when social forces require us to do more, to do it better, and to do it with less, as we are faced with

- growth in demand for resources and simultaneous constraints on their availability;
- greater consumer advocacy and expectations of accountability;
- an increasing need and drive for higher education institutions to become integral parts of their communities, while learning how to specifically meet community needs; and

- an evolving policy domain that is shaping and redirecting higher education goals and initiatives.

Higher education is frequently declared to be "in crisis," government is concerned with reinventing itself, our health system is changing every day (despite the supposed failure of national health reform), and, in general, society seems to be concerned with doing better with less. There is a lot of tension in the system — and when we try to address these tensions we recognize that there is an urgent need to do something. This is commencement time nationwide, and we could look at any set of graduates and ask whether they are prepared and positioned to deal with this tension-filled environment: Are the new teachers prepared for the challenges of the diminishing funding

This turbulent environment suggests the need to do something – and one part of doing something is to think about how we can do a better job of knowing what we are doing in higher education.

● ●

of the public school system? Are the new doctors ready to work in a managed-care environment? Do the new public administration graduates understand what public service means today? Do public health graduates really understand the "public" part of health? We want to do better at what we do, but we are not necessarily sure of how to approach that improvement.

This is an era of change. We see tensions for change in higher education and tensions for change in accreditation. I currently serve as project director for the Task Force on Accreditation of Health Professions Education, supported by the Pew Charitable Trusts, and based at the Center for the Health Professions at the University of California at San Francisco (Task Force 1996). Some of you may have encountered the work of the Pew Health Professions Commission, also based at the center, which has been studying health professions education and workforce issues in this country for the past nine years and has made a series of policy recommendations, many of which have already been implemented (see Shugars, O'Neil, and Bader 1991; O'Neil 1993; Pew Health Professions

Tensions in Higher Education

Degree focus	←——→	Lifelong learning
Campus setting	←——→	Computer network
Classes	←——→	Individualized learning
Lecture pedagogy	←→	Multimedia presentations
Reputation	←——→	Price
Traditional students	←——→	Adult learners
Western culture	←——→	Multicultural
Homogeneous student body	←—→	Diverse student body
Unidisciplinary	←——→	Multidisciplinary
Unrestricted giving	←——→	Targeted giving

Commission 1995).

As part of our Task Force work, we have attempted to articulate some of these tensions in the system (Task Force 1996-97).

Complementing these tensions in higher education are a similar set of tensions in accreditation. Few topics in higher education engender as much debate and emotion as that of accreditation. There has been extensive debate for many years in higher education circles about the role and value of accreditation. At the same time, there has been nearly constant study of accreditation and frequent organization and reorganization of the systems for monitoring, evaluating, recognizing, certifying, and accrediting educational programs,

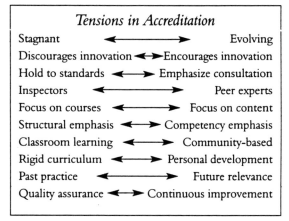

Tensions in Accreditation

Stagnant	←——→	Evolving
Discourages innovation	←→	Encourages innovation
Hold to standards	←——→	Emphasize consultation
Inspectors	←——→	Peer experts
Focus on courses	←——→	Focus on content
Structural emphasis	←→	Competency emphasis
Classroom learning	←——→	Community-based
Rigid curriculum	←——→	Personal development
Past practice	←——→	Future relevance
Quality assurance	←→	Continuous improvement

resulting in a continuing state of unrest and discontent. We have identified this set of tensions in accreditation (Task Force 1996-97):

In the accreditation community, there has been additional dissonance since the early 1990s, beginning with concerns raised during the reauthorization of the Higher Education Act and continuing through the dissolution in 1993 of the Council on Postsecondary Accreditation (COPA). During this time, many of the specialized and professional accreditors came to realize that they had professional and organizational needs that would not be met with the disappearance of COPA. Under the leadership of the elected officials of the Assembly of Specialized Accrediting Bodies within COPA, a new organization was established in 1993 to address specifically the needs of specialized and professional accrediting agencies. This new organization, the Association of Specialized and Professional Accreditors (ASPA), became an important facilitator for developing common practices for specialized and professional accreditation and for sharing information within this community (see, for example, ASPA, 1993, 1995). Today, ASPA continues to be an effective resource for the specialized accrediting community, and it is working with the new Council on Higher Education Accreditation (CHEA) to address common visions for accreditation.

This turbulent environment suggests the need to do something — and one part of doing something is to think about how we can do a better job of knowing what we are doing in higher education. My professional career has been spent working in the health system, so I will rely heavily on this background to draw general illustrations about how our system today positions us to think about improvement.

How can we move to our desired future for higher education? I do not presume to be able to make a diagnosis and recommend a treatment plan that will solve all the ills of higher education. My charge in this talk is to introduce the strand of this AAHE meeting that will focus on accreditation and to suggest ways in which accreditation and assessment might be more closely integrated to achieve what I am calling "intentional improvement" — improvement that is the result of a clear plan and that results in desirable changes.

My intent is to explore the following points:
● the relationship of assessment and accreditation;
● whether accreditation is, in fact, a structured process of assessment;
● what the linkage is to an ongoing and deliberate strategy for improvement;
● the perception that accreditation is disconnected from improvement;
● the accreditation/assessment process as a

fundamental component of ongoing program development and review; and
● the reconceptualization of accreditation as an intention to improve.

ASSESSMENT, ACCREDITATION, AND IMPROVEMENT: THE CONCEPTS

I assume a high level of understanding by this audience about these basic concepts, but it nonetheless might be useful to set a context.

Assessment programs enable academic units to focus on indicators and measures such as student learning outcomes, program evaluation, and institutional effectiveness, in order to improve the quality of teaching and learning (Gelmon, Reagan, and Merrill 1996). Accreditation is used for purposes of external recognition, eligibility for federal support, and articulation with professional regulation. Assessment may be driven by internal mandates, with no clear standards or framework for activities; accreditation assures minimum standards of performance, to ensure that practitioners are capable of meeting at least the minimum threshold of acceptable practice. Improvement allows us to reframe assessment and accreditation as activities for intentional improvement — we engage because we have a clear aim of improvement. Assessment offers internal systematic analysis of activities; accreditation validates the standards of performance and assures a baseline level of uniform quality across comparable programs or institutions. When viewing these as linked activities that are part of intentional improvement, we can begin to work on setting and achieving "stretch" goals that move us toward excellence and link activities with our overall aims (Gelmon, Sinioris, and Najafi 1995).

Assessment
In talking about assessment, I believe that we are addressing three major concepts:
● a process of collecting, organizing, and

interpreting data;

- the determination as to what degree the educational program meets the established mission, goals, and objectives; and
- the measurement and evaluation of outcomes related to performance, efforts, or accomplishments.

We often speak of assessment strictly in terms of assessment of student outcomes; I have found it valuable to consider a broader approach in which we consider assessment as a global process that can also be applied to faculty, programs, and institutions (Gelmon and Reagan 1995). In 1991, Pat Hutchings, Ted Marchese, and Barbara Wright (1991) commented that assessment should be valued not only for the data it produces but also for the processes it fosters and stimulates. I wish we could say the same about accreditation — but there are few opportunities to do so.

Accreditation

I could assume a common understanding among you of what is meant by "accreditation," but often I encounter mixed perceptions of what accreditation is and how it works in the U.S. system of higher education. Accreditation exists as a means of assuring the public of educational program quality; of promoting continuing review and self-improvement by educational units in preparation for accreditation reviews; and more important, of facilitating integrated, continuous assessment, evaluation, and improvement (see, for example, Filerman 1984; Gelmon 1995; Millard 1984). In general, accreditation

- is a voluntary, nongovernmental process;
- is based upon guided self-evaluation and self-improvement;
- relies upon peer review, which in turn stimulates evaluation and program management; and
- judges the effectiveness of the academic unit against a set of predetermined standards.

Accreditation as we know it consists of a series of common activities:

- self-study
- preparation of documentation
- on-site peer evaluation
- report
- accreditation decision
- periodic review and reporting.

Variation across accreditation agencies is evident when one looks at specific procedures — length of time between site visits, composition of the site-visit team, expectations for documentation — but in general, all of the recognized agencies (both regional and specialized) employ these common activities. The system of guided self-evaluation and self-improvement stimulated by accreditation is central to this voluntary effort at self-regulation. The primary value of accreditation can be found not in the outcomes, but rather in the process of evaluation and program management stimulated by this peer review (Gelmon forthcoming). The effectiveness of accreditation may be judged by its ability to encourage and promote programs and institutions to evaluate their educational activities and to use the evaluation results for ongoing improvement to better meet customer needs.

As a point-in-time review, accreditation, as we know it today, has difficulty accommodating the natural process of program evolution. This difficulty is perceived by some as presenting a barrier to innovation and creativity because of the rigidity of the accreditation format and its need to keep procedures consistent for at least a period of years in order to ensure comparability of reviews across academic units over time. This rigid application of standards and procedures may not be in tune with current educational methods or professional practice. As a result, the perception exists that accreditation limits changes and innovations in curriculum and program delivery (Bender 1983).

Accreditation thus provides benefits to various "publics," including the following:

- advances/enhances the profession or discipline;
- supports access to the profession or

discipline;
- facilitates professional mobility;
- supports individual credentialing processes;
- provides consumer protection; and
- affords opportunities for educational funding. (see, for example, ASPA 1993, 1995)

Improvement

The third major concept is that of improvement and of understanding the difference between traditional improvement and continual improvement.

Traditionally, we assumed professional knowledge of the subject, the discipline, and its related values and therefore worked on traditional improvement. Continual improvement is based on Deming's theory of profound knowledge — a knowledge of systems, an understanding of variation, an application of psychology, and a theory of knowledge (Batalden and Stoltz 1993). It is the linkage of traditional improvement with continual improvement that provides leverage for conceptualizing our work — in particular, when we are assessing professions or disciplines and need that expert knowledge base as well as improvement knowledge. Improvement comes from the application of this knowledge. The "Model for Improvement" proposed by Langley, Nolan, and Nolan (1994) provides a framework within which to gain and apply knowledge for the improvement of a wide variety of endeavors — processes, products, services, programs, work patterns, personal life, etc. It consists of three fundamental questions derived from the work of W. Edwards Deming:
- *Aim:* What are we trying to accomplish?
- *Current Knowledge:* How will we know that a change is an improvement?
- *Cycle for Improvement:* What changes can we make that will result in improvement?

These questions help us to focus our efforts on thinking about learning as our primary

We often speak of assessment strictly in terms of assessment of student outcomes; I have found it valuable to consider a broader approach in which we consider assessment as a global process that can also be applied to faculty, programs, and institutions.

● ●

aim. But we need to recognize that there are different types of learning and different contexts for learning. The university is given responsibility by society to foster and stimulate learning as the primary focus toward which all efforts are concentrated. Thus the emphasis is on the student who is learning, on the faculty who are learning and contributing to new knowledge, on institutional learning, and on learning with the community to ensure that learning is relevant to the local context. I am constantly reminded of these differences as I compare the urban university where I work, where teaching is the primary mission, with those universities where I studied, which were driven by the academic health center and its research mission. I also see the differences in learning when I consider undergraduate general education programs, as compared with graduate professional programs. Our common aim is learning, but how the learning occurs may differ.

Systematic improvement efforts incorporate the documentation of the strength and vitality of programs. Well-designed and executed assessment programs — which may be part of self-study efforts in preparation for accreditation or may be routine program monitoring — will yield information about the strengths and weaknesses of academic units and the relationships among structures, processes, and outcomes (Gelmon and Reagan 1995). The information obtained from such assessments yields information helpful in identifying opportunities, dealing with challenges, revising aims and goals, and allocating resources wisely. Conducting such appraisals from a systems perspective attends to both outcomes and processes, so that linkages can

In industry, change takes months, but in academe, it can take years — so can we create opportunities to use the model for improvement while implementing rapid change?

●●●●●●●●●●●●●●●●●●●●●●●●●●●●●●●●●●●●

be made to environmental factors as well as internal issues. Integrating assessment, evaluation, and improvement can help to build a common, shared educational vision whereby participants — both the providers and the consumers of the educational products — collectively embrace the organizational goals.

ACCOUNTABILITY

What drives us to commit so much energy to thinking about mechanisms for improvement such as assessment and accreditation? Demands for accountability are increasing in the higher education community. Self-regulation, which is one of the essential foundations of the U.S. system of accreditation in higher education, may need to be redefined within the context of its mission of consumer protection. Peter Ewell (1994) has advocated assurance to the community of academic quality; this requires a focus on the assessment of outcomes and the active use of results, with particular attention being paid to evaluating a student's competencies in order to ensure the knowledge, skills, and other attributes students seek from their academic experience. Ewell suggests that greater attention to the use of results may be needed not only for accreditation but also to regain public confidence in higher education. Accreditation agencies need to be acutely aware of the need to maintain public confidence, given that accreditation is "voluntary," and to ensure that they enjoy the continuing confidence of accreditation's many publics. Institutions of higher education face the same issue of confidence.

When considering educational improvement, we need to assume the perspective of the customer — and there may be multiple customers. Some of my favorite examples of applying the customer perspective come from

health services. For example, many of you will have been a patient in a health care organization at some point and have been frustrated by the experience — dealing with multiple hand-offs, an endless stream of different specialized providers, each responsible for only a small portion of your care, a lack of information, unnecessary waits and delays, rude service. We often see the greatest improvements in patient care when we ask primary care providers and administrators to live the experience of the patient. Another example is the person who comes to the hospital for a treadmill test and ends up walking more miles through the hospital during the various steps of pretest screening than when actually on the treadmill (Bisognano 1997). The frustrations these experiences engender clearly identify opportunities for improvement. In education, we can play the role of the student and see what the process is like — whether it be admissions, advising, career counseling, preparation for graduation — and then become convinced of the need for more experimentation with changes to improve processes, consume less time, use fewer forms, and generally enhance process flow.

MOVING TO IMPROVEMENT

The model for improvement provides a useful framework for thinking about the reconceptualization of assessment and accreditation as improvement activities — What is the purpose of the work? Where should the focus of these reviews be? How might we create change? How might these changes be tested? What opportunities can be created for experimentation with minimal risk? In industry, change takes months, but in academe, it can take years — so can we create opportunities to use the model for improvement to implement rapid change? This should be possible if we use improvement knowledge to accelerate our work, based on the subject knowledge of our professions and our disciplines.

The model allows tests of change, while accommodating the need to gain more knowledge before developing a particular change. The third question sets up the opportunity for tests of change — to demonstrate the improvement, increase knowledge to develop a change, make tests, and then implement the change itself (Langley, Nolan, and Nolan 1994). It uses the Plan-Do-Study-Act approach (PDSA), sometimes called the Deming or Shewhart cycle, and it consists of the following steps:

- *Plan:* State the objective of the test; make predictions; develop a plan to carry out the test (who, what, where, when, how).

- *Do:* Carry out the test; document problems and unexpected observations; begin analysis of the data.

- *Study:* Complete the analysis of the data; compare test data with predictions; summarize what was learned.

- *Act:* What changes are to be made? What will be the objective of the next cycle?

We can run these small tests of change in our daily work and readily integrate improvement, let alone building it into more long-term assessment activities. We conduct organizational assessments, but how do we know that the standards we have set are the right ones? We engage in more deliberate review and inquiry, such as through the Baldrige self-assessment process. The PDSA approach can become the model for assessment of routine, ongoing activities that are part of our daily work. Preparation for accreditation then becomes a summation of the multiple tests of change, with documented evidence of what has been done, why, what improvements have been made, and what the focus is for subsequent work.

Change is helpful, but at the same time needs to be made in a controlled manner. The traditional lengthy, diagnostic journey of quality improvement, which many of you may have engaged in at your institutions, is increasingly viewed as excessive in today's world — spending months in diagnosis with no improvements. We cannot afford that sort of time expenditure today — the problems just will not wait. It is like conducting a course evaluation at the end of the course — useful for the professor for the next offering of the course, but providing no opportunity for making improvements that will benefit the current students. Rapid-cycle tests of change would allow the professor to make improvements throughout the course and thereby benefit the current students, as well as developing knowledge for future courses. Some of these approaches may be familiar to you under the umbrella of "classroom assessment techniques" — strategies articulated by colleagues such as Tom Angelo and Pat Cross, which have accelerated learning in the application of improvement theory in higher education.

THE NEED FOR ARTICULATION OF ASSESSMENT AND ACCREDITATION

Can accreditation become a model for assessment and improvement? I believe that it can — and that a closer articulation of assessment methods and accreditation will greatly enhance our efforts toward educational improvement. The focus on improvement is not intended to suggest that there is nothing good about accreditation today, but rather to focus attention on how it can become better. Why has there not been more reform in the systems of accreditation of education? Perhaps because accreditors and educators have been reluctant to experiment and take risks, given the attacks on accreditation that have been prevalent in higher education during the past two decades. Why is there so much discontent and resistance to change by the stakeholders in accreditation? Perhaps because those working in accreditation on a day-to-day basis are consumed with detail and routine tasks, and are subsequently unable to free themselves for long-range strategic thinking about the overall process of accreditation. Similarly, for many, assessment is a new concept, and they are just beginning to embark upon comprehensive assessment programs. Together this creates an atmosphere where there has been little effort devoted to thinking about how to articulate assessment and accreditation. How, then, can improvement and change be accomplished?

A MODEL FOR IMPLEMENTING CHANGE IN EDUCATION

In most industries, change happens regardless of whether one is eager for, or resistant to, it. In education and in accreditation, resistance to change is often sufficiently intense to inhibit or actually stifle new ideas. Yet successful change can be a positive activity. To champion change in the face of resistance requires commitment and energy. In preparing for this presentation, I studied some recent work on change and improvement and have applied it to thinking about assessment and accreditation. One particularly useful resource was *The Improvement Guide* (Langley et al. 1997).

Any approach to improvement must be based on building and applying knowledge; actual improvements will only happen as a result of that application of knowledge. If one applies the Model for Improvement, described earlier, we need to answer the basic questions of that model. What are we trying to accomplish — what is the aim of the improvement effort that will guide and keep the assessment and accreditation effort focused? The aim is to respond to many of the issues identified as weaknesses of the current accreditation process: cost, duplication, excessive focus on inspection, limitation on innovation, redundancy of the processes built into the accreditation system.

How will we know that a change is an improvement? One measure will be the increased satisfaction of the customers of education — whether these are students, community members, institutional administrators, faculty, professional leadership, or other concerned individuals and groups. A second measure might relate to changes in the political climate, such that there are fewer perceived "attacks" on accreditation and more support for the concepts and principles advocated by it. In general, the effectiveness of the change will be judged by the ability to determine criteria for success and to measure the impact of the change. Perhaps the most evident change would be when individuals engage in assessment on a routine basis and anticipate accreditation eagerly because it is a value-added activity that enhances their work, rather than a burdensome exercise that consumes resources with little return.

Finally, what changes can be made that will result in an improvement? There are many possibilities for change, but they will require new ways of thinking about how we evaluate higher education and how we approach our daily work — and they will challenge the current system. These changes will demand that leaders in higher education — including accreditors and their key stakeholders — begin to operate within a mode of flexibility and adaptability, rather than rigidity and conformance to history.

STRATEGIES FOR SUPPORTING AND SUSTAINING IMPROVEMENT

The Task Force on Accreditation of Health Professions Education has generated a series of questions that we believe need to be answered in order to consider reforms in accreditation and its role as a mechanism for assessment and improvement (1996-97). Some key questions to be addressed in developing strategies include these:

- To whom are accreditors accountable?
- Does accreditation promote improve-

ment, or does it focus solely on compliance?

- Does accreditation facilitate effective working relationships among stakeholders?
- Does accreditation provide the assurance of quality education that it is expected to provide?
- Does accreditation really make a difference?

The following discussion highlights some key areas where new strategies for accreditation might move us toward a system of "intentional improvement," in which the assessment system accommodates the current realities of a resource-constrained environment, uses data wisely and frugally, is based on an understanding of the systems of education and accreditation, acknowledges inevitable variation, and fosters innovation and creativity. The intent is not to denigrate the many positive aspects of accreditation as it exists today, recognizing the individual strengths and the variability across different accrediting agencies, but rather to build upon the community's collective wisdom to strengthen accreditation and make it a more effective force in promoting the quality of higher education. Perhaps these strategies will stimulate thought about actions that are realistic and practical and that will seed changes and improvements.

Utilization of Data

Many accreditation systems are consumed with collecting data but have no system for synthesizing and analyzing that data once collected. This constrains improvement efforts, because there are no possibilities to test changes and demonstrate the effects of those changes. There is little, if any, precedent for experiments in accreditation. What if the experiment fails? What would be the implications for the program/school in terms of accreditation status, professional stature, eligibility for federal funding, etc.? This is a risk that accreditation agencies have been unwilling or unable to take. Unfortunately, an

There are many possibilities for change, but they will require new ways of thinking about how we evaluate higher education and how we approach our daily work – and they will challenge the current system.

● ●

inspection mentality has perpetuated in some accreditation systems, looking at lists, numbers, and quantitative measures. What do these tell us about quality?

Frequently, data are collected as a historical practice. Accreditation could help academic units by focusing on the assessment process, whereby goals, objectives, and desired outcomes are clearly articulated; only then should measures be developed and data collected that become the means for assessing achievement of outcomes. Simply setting out to collect data can cause change to occur because of the inevitable awareness of a process that develops from trying to measure it. The act of measurement can be the trigger to move a process toward the desired results. This brings the work of routine assessment in line with information collection necessary for accreditation, and it permits ongoing consideration of the information, rather than periodic review in the midst of a flurry of activity as a self-study is prepared.

One of the activities of our task force has been to review many of the sets of accrediting standards from a range of accreditors (Berkman and Gelmon 1997). Our findings illustrate the continuing dependence on data — reams of paper, pages of tables, and the uncertain utility of this information. Each data item suggests that we ask questions such as

- What difference does it make if we have this piece of information?
- How much effort is required to collect it?
- Will it be used?
- What does it really tell us?

The uses of information collected in the accreditation process also merit attention. Academic units collect extensive data, present

The accreditor should be less focused on the process and more focused on the outcomes, asking questions such as, "Is the graduate competent and prepared to enter professional practice in the specific field?"

● ●

them in various formats depending on the requirements of the accreditation (or other evaluating) entity, and often do not revisit the information. Given the extensive effort needed to assemble this information, it would seem logical that academic units would then collect and update this information on a regular basis in order to use it for routine program monitoring, evaluation, and improvement. Yet this does not happen. Perhaps this is due to the data collection format being cumbersome, or there being no person or other mechanism to routinely collect and document the information, or decision makers not knowing what to do with the information. This suggests a need for greater articulation between the "evidence collection" aspect of accreditation and routine program assessment and improvement on the part of the academic units. This also lends credence to the argument that accreditation systems should coordinate their data collection needs and streamline their formats to permit a unified information base at each university from which the data necessary for a focused accreditation review can be extracted. This would require collaboration between the institutional and specialized accreditors; it might decrease the reporting burden and increase overall satisfaction with the multiple accrediting processes taking place on individual campuses.

Understanding the Systems of Education and Accreditation

A frequent complaint about accreditation — and particularly about specialized and programmatic accreditation — is that the focus on a specific profession or discipline is presented as being self-serving and myopic and that there is no recognition of the larger system in which the specialized program operates.

Accreditors have been known to demand changes in institutional policies that are not within the purview of the individual program. This leads to questions of the relevance of the individual review if it does not acknowledge the larger governing system. Professions have an established body of knowledge, and as a result, some translate this professional domain into a tightly constrained approach to accreditation, not taking into account that there may be considerable diversity across institutions in how they deliver their educational programs. The accreditor should be less focused on the process (which may reveal innovative ways of overcoming barriers) and more focused on the outcomes, asking questions such as, "Is the graduate competent and prepared to enter professional practice in the specific field?" Yet, accreditors devote enormous resources to examining discrete aspects of the process and often appear to be less concerned with graduate competencies and other program outcomes. This suggests a need for accreditation evaluations to be vested in examining programs in the context of specific institutional and programmatic missions, and to emphasize outcomes and competencies rather than structures and processes. Again, this presents an opportunity to link assessment with accreditation practices.

Concepts of Variation

Accreditation is ill-equipped to deal with normal variation, yet variation exists in all aspects of any process. There are variations in systems, in processes, in institutions, and in people. Similarly, the means by which a specific activity will be conducted and completed will vary across the individuals and organizations leading the activity, no matter how tightly proscribed. Variation in an activity may reflect a fundamental change, or it may be a normal occurrence that reflects a random change, leaving the underlying systems intact. Problems occur in the accreditation process when such random change is viewed as a fundamental change, causing extensive effort —

effort to remedy the situation when, in fact, no effort is necessary other than understanding that such variation does occur from time to time and dealing with the immediate consequences. Accreditors would be well served if they could be prepared to identify such random variation and to learn from these events without imposing punishment or additional reporting on the academic unit. This variation should not be ignored, but it needs to be recognized and accommodated.

Innovation and Creativity

Critics of accreditation would suggest that the term "accreditation innovation" is an oxymoron. Yet the study of creativity and creative thinking reveals some practical applications that could reform systems of accreditation and approaches to accreditation without much effort (Langley et al. 1996). The following are some suggestions for stimulating accreditation innovation:

● *Challenge the boundaries:* Real reform of accreditation will occur when boundaries and barriers are expanded or eliminated through creative new methods and approaches.

● *Rearrange the order of the steps:* The process of accreditation should be broken down into the individual activities, and then serious consideration should be given to reordering the process of these activities to identify opportunities for change.

● *Look for ways to smooth the flow of activities:* Multiple hurdles and obstacles appear throughout the accreditation process, and it may be possible to identify mechanisms at the level of both the local program and the accrediting agency itself to improve, streamline, and smooth the flow.

● *Evaluate the purpose:* As stated above, much of the accreditation process is accepted as historical process or because it has never

been questioned. A careful examination of the reasons for the various inputs, processes, and outputs of an accreditation system may reveal steps that can be eliminated if they are not vital to the purpose.

● *Visualize the ideal:* Accreditors and the accredited should engage in discussions about the ideal situation for accreditation. The task force has asked some audiences whether health professions education could exist without specialized accreditation. Similar discussions could take place to help concerned stakeholders articulate the true value of accreditation and the ideal system for making it operational.

● *Remove "the current way of doing things" as an option:* If the current system is no longer considered a viable alternative, there will be no choice but to identify new ways to conduct accreditation. Exploring such alternatives may generate concepts and methods that will be more suited to the purposes for which accreditation was designed.

Creating a culture of innovation will shift the emphasis of accreditation. Some accreditors have viewed themselves only as evaluators and standard setters; their role as consultants, peer coaches, and advisers has been minimal — driven perhaps by the need to maintain objectivity and fulfill the "separate and independent" requirement from the U.S. Department of Education. Others have been able to engage in considerable consultation and thus demonstrate value to their constituents in ways in addition to evaluation.

HOW WE MIGHT MAKE CHANGE

Change concepts have recently been introduced into the improvement literature by Langley et al. (1996) as a lever for provoking new ideas, new methods, and new approaches. By themselves, the concepts do not suggest the strategies for improvement. Rather, they serve as the basis to consider a situation — in this context, accreditation of higher education — and from there can be turned into ideas that can be made operational in order to achieve improvement. Langley et al. suggest an initial list of seventy change concepts, derived from their work on improvement in a variety of industries. These concepts can be grouped into nine categories of change as follows; a sample change concept relevant to accreditation is attached to each:

- focus on the product or service — differentiate products using quality dimensions;
- design systems to avoid mistakes — set reminders;
- eliminate waste — reduce controls on the system;
- manage time — reduce setup or startup time;
- manage variation — stop tampering;
- improve workflow — move steps in the process closer together;
- change the work environment — give people access to information;
- enhance the producer/customer relationship — focus on the outcome to a customer; and
- optimize inventory — reduce multiple brands of the same item.

The intent of thinking about change concepts is to stimulate thinking about improvement in a new way. Instead of focusing on what is "wrong" with accreditation, these categories of concepts help us to focus on areas where change might be feasible. Accreditors can benchmark their efforts for change and improvement against other industries where such efforts have been successful, they can learn from experiences in other contexts, and then they can apply the lessons in a manner relevant to their specific activities. However, to successfully benchmark, one needs to understand one's own organization as a basis for comparisons. Change is not impossible in accreditation, but there needs to be a ground-swell of interest in order for change to be stimulated, to be forward-thinking, and to come from within rather than being imposed by an external body.

SOME PRACTICAL WAYS OF THINKING ABOUT CHANGE

I have recently had the opportunity to work with a new tool called the "value compass" as a way of considering an activity to help assess its value, identify areas for improvement, and focus improvement activities to ensure they address value. Just as a traditional compass is used to verify location and identify the direction in which you want to travel, the value compass assists us in assessing and identifying opportunities for improvement. This tool is modified from the clinical value compass developed by Eugene Nelson and Paul Batalden of the Center for the Evaluative Clinical Sciences at Dartmouth Medical School (see Nelson, Batalden, and Mohr 1996). It is now being tested in applications for education through the early work of Linda Norman (1997) at Vanderbilt University's School of Nursing and the participants in the Community-Based Quality Improvement in Education for the Health Professions Collaborative, sponsored by the Institute for Healthcare Improvement and by the Bureau of Health Professions of the U.S. Public Health Service.

Consider an educational program or experience that you want to assess. Begin to the west with learning objectives/course outcomes — accomplishment of the desired outcomes would be your entry on the compass. Then move north to overall professional competencies/outcomes — here your measurements could include student perceptions of levels of accomplishment, as well as faculty perceptions, with respect to terminal competency. To the east is satisfaction — how satisfied are faculty, students, or employers with the student outcomes? Finally, move south to cost — costs of faculty and student time, resources used, credit hours or tuition generated. Put this information together, and you begin to see relationships among the components, which quickly leads to identification of opportunities for improvement.

Another useful way of thinking about a problem and trying to identify the leverage points for improvement is to use the concept triangle, one of the tools for creative thinking offered by Edward DeBono (see Ross 1997). The three points of the triangle are identified as *problem, idea, concept.* Once again, a health care illustration is useful. A major problem in hospitals relates to the management of operating rooms, which are frequently plagued by delays in start times for surgery, which then back up the subsequent schedule. The problem is delays in start times; the idea is to provide a beeper to the surgeon to ensure he or she comes to the operating suite when the surgery is ready to begin; the concept is to synchronize the work of all the players involved. The challenge is that there are multiple perspectives of the concept — the nurse believes the activity starts when he or she begins to set up the operating room; the anesthesiologist believes the activity starts when he or she starts the flow of anesthetic; and the surgeon believes the activity starts when he or she makes the first incision. For all three, the problem and the idea are the same, but the concept is different. Think of the graduate student who is processing his or her paperwork for graduation and experiences what appear to be unexplained delays in the process. The student thinks the process its done when he or she submits the graduation papers; the adviser thinks it is done when signing off on the forms; the department administrator thinks it is done when she sends it to Graduate Studies; but Graduate Studies doesn't even think the process has begun until it receives the paperwork — which has already been processed by multiple individuals. If we put this in perspective, looking at the concept triangle, we begin to see how various attempts at improvement may make no difference until

> ## We need to create a culture where innovation is rewarded and where creative change in short time frames is encouraged.

we deal with the fundamental concept that is the issue.

CONCLUSION

There are many opportunities for improvement in higher education, and we can streamline some of this work by more carefully articulating the evaluative activities we conduct under the auspices of both assessment and accreditation. This effort can be enhanced by drawing upon improvement knowledge and by adapting some of the methods being used in other industries to identify opportunities for improvement, develop tests of change, run small experiments, and use the resulting knowledge to make lasting improvements. We need to create a culture where innovation is rewarded and where creative change in short time frames is encouraged. Through closer alignment of our internal assessment systems, and the external reviews conducted by various accreditation agencies, we can consolidate many of our efforts and focus our work — and our utilization of precious resources — on making incremental changes to improve our systems of higher education and better prepare our graduates for productive roles in our society.

I anticipate that some of the themes of this presentation will be picked up in the various sessions that follow within this strand on accreditation, and I look forward to the continuing discussions of how we can link assessment and accreditation to create intentional improvement. ◆

REFERENCES

Association of Specialized and Professional Accreditors. *Code of Good Practice: A Policy*

Statement. Chicago: ASPA, 1995.

――――― . *The Role and Value of Specialized Accreditation: A Policy Statement.* Arlington, VA: ASPA, 1993.

Baker, G. Ross. Presentation to the Community-Based Quality Improvement in Education for the Health Professions Collaborative. Cleveland, June 1997.

Batalden, Paul B., and Patricia K. Stoltz. "A Framework for the Continual Improvement of Health Care: Building and Applying Professional and Improvement Knowledge to Test Changes in Daily Work." *Joint Commission Journal of Quality Improvement* 19 (October 1993): 424-47.

Bender, Louis W. "Accreditation: Misuses and Misconceptions." In *Understanding Accreditation,* edited by Kenneth E. Young et al., pp.71-85. San Francisco: Jossey-Bass, 1983.

Berkman, Akiko M., and Sherril B. Gelmon. "Common Themes in Contemporary Accreditation Standards." Working Paper for the Task Force on Accreditation of Health Professions Education. UCSF Center for the Health Professions, 1997.

Bisognano, Maureen. Presentation to the Community-Based Quality Improvement in Education for the Health Professions Collaborative. Cleveland, June 1997.

Ewell, Peter T. "A Matter of Integrity: Accountability and the Future of Self-Regulation." *Change* 26 (November/December 1994): 24-29.

Filerman, Gary L. "The Influence of Policy Objectives on Professional Education and Accreditation: The Case of Hospital Accreditation." *Journal of Health Administration Education* 2 (Fall 1984): 409-18.

Gelmon, Sherril B. "Accreditation, Core Curriculum, and Allied Health Education: Barriers and Opportunities." *Journal of Allied Health,* forthcoming.

――――― . "Accreditation as a Stimulus for Continuous Improvement in Health Management Education: A Case Study of ACEHSA." Fellowship thesis, American College of Healthcare Executives, 1995.

Gelmon, Sherril B., and Janet T. Reagan. *Assessment in a Quality Improvement Framework: A Sourcebook for Health Administration Education.* Arlington, VA: Association of University Programs in Health Administration, 1995.

Gelmon, Sherril B., Janet T. Reagan, and Ronald B. Merrill. "Assessment in a Quality Improvement Framework: Applications in Health Administration Education." *Journal of Health Administration Education* 14 (Fall 1996): 473-97.

Gelmon, Sherril B., Marie E. Sinioris, and Kevin L. Najafi. "Performance Assessment for Health Administration Education: Applications of the Baldrige Criteria." *Journal of Health Administration Education* 13 (Winter 1995): 109-27.

Hutchings, P., T. Marchese, and B. Wright. *Using Assessment to Strengthen General Education.* Washington, DC: AAHE, 1991.

Langley, Gerald J., Kevin M. Nolan, and Thomas W. Nolan. "The Foundation of Improvement." *Quality Progress* (June 1994): 81-86.

Langley, G. J., K. M. Nolan, T. W. Nolan, C. L. Norman, and L. P. Provost. *The Improvement Guide: A Practical Approach to Enhancing Organizational Performance.* San Francisco: Jossey-Bass, 1996.

Millard, Richard M. "The Structure of

Specialized Accreditation in the United States." *Journal of Education for Library and Information Science* 25 (Fall 1984): 87-97.

Nelson, Eugene, Paul B. Batalden, and Julie Mohr. "The Clinical Value Compass." Unpublished documents, Center for the Evaluative Clinical Sciences, Dartmouth University Medical School, 1996.

Norman, Linda. "Applications of the Value Compass in Professional Education." Presentation to the Community-Based Quality Improvement in Education for the Health Professions Collaborative. Cleveland, June 1997.

O'Neil, Edward H. *Health Professions Education for the Future: Schools in Service to the Nation.* San Francisco: Pew Health Professions Commission, 1993.

Pew Health Professions Commission. *Critical Challenges: Revitalizing the Health Professions for the Twenty-First Century.* San Francisco: UCSF Center for the Health Professions, 1995.

Shugars, D. A., E. H. O'Neil, and J. D. Bader. *Healthy America: Practitioners for 2005, An Agenda for Action for U.S. Health Professional Schools.* Durham, NC: Pew Health Professions Commission, 1991.

Task Force on Accreditation of Health Professions Education. Working papers, UCSF Center for the Health Professions, 1996-97.

———. "Backgrounder." San Francisco: UCSF Center for the Health Professions, 1996.

Sherril B. Gelmon is associate professor of public health at Portland State University, PO Box 751-PA, Portland, OR 97207-0751, sherril@upa.pdx.edu.

I t is a privilege to introduce the 1997 conference strand featuring the contributions of out-of-class experiences to student learning and personal development. My interest in life outside the classroom dates back more than thirty years. My college transcripts prove it! And what was a source of great satisfaction to me as an undergraduate

Working Together to Enhance Student Learning Inside and Outside the Classroom

BY GEORGE KUH

evolved into an interesting line of scholarship these past two decades.

For the first few years of this work, I felt like a Don Quixote, tilting at windmills. Few others seemed to be interested in what students did with their time after class. But within the last few years, a lot of evidence has shown that what students do outside the classroom influences what and how much they learn (see Astin 1993; Baxter Magolda 1992; Chickering and Reisser 1993; Kuh 1993, 1995; Kuh et al. 1997, 1994, 1991; Pace 1990; Pascarella and Terenzini 1991; Terenzini, Pascarella, and Blimling 1996). For example, it's now clear that intellectual and cognitive development are not the exclusive province of so-called "academic" or in-class tasks, but are associated with a variety of social as well as

intellectual experiences (Kuh 1995; Pascarella and Terenzini 1991; Terenzini et al. 1995a. 1995b). Examples of such activities are studying, using information resources including the library, interacting with peers and faculty, participating in formal programs and informal campus-based events (e.g., orientation, cultural and theatrical performances) and activities (e.g., organizations), working on or off the campus, and using other human (instructors, advisers, coaches, administrators) and physical (unions, playing fields, residences) resources that colleges provide for undergraduate learning and personal development.

When in-class and out-of-class experiences are mutually supportive — what I call "seamless learning" — students gain more from their college experience (Kuh 1996; Kuh et al.

Contact with people with diverse perspectives or those who have more advanced stages of moral reasoning appear to enhance [students'] moral reasoning abilities and identity formation.

● ●

1991; Pascarella and Terenzini 1991). Certain features of the institution can be intentionally arranged to achieve this complementarity, thereby influencing — at least to a degree — the amount of effort students devote to activities that matter to their education. And quality of effort is the single best predictor of learning outcomes (Astin 1993; Pace 1990).

The idea of getting students to devote more of their out-of-class time to educationally purposeful activities has been around a long time. It's not likely to go away. Employers, legislators, family members, and students themselves want to be sure college graduates have the skills and competencies required by the workplace of the future, what Bruffee (1993:1) called "the craft of interdependence." These skills include oral and written communication, group process, teamwork, decision making, and understanding the workplace culture (Ewell 1994). Although such competencies can be obtained in classrooms, the nature of many out-of-class activities often *requires* that students become competent in these areas (Kuh 1995). This is because many experiences outside the classroom put the student at the center of learning (Baxter Magolda 1994), demanding that students test their skills and values in situations not unlike those they will encounter after college.

The rest of this paper is divided into three parts. First, I'll briefly review some of the contributions of out-of-class experiences to selected outcomes of college. Then, I'll discuss the Student Learning Imperative (American College Personnel Association 1994), which is being used to promote collaboration between the two groups who spend

the most time with students — faculty and student affairs staff. Such collaboration is essential to help students make meaning of their in-class and out-of-class experiences, thereby increasing the amount they learn. I'll close with some ways institutions are pursuing the seamless learning agenda.

STUDENT LEARNING OUTSIDE THE CLASSROOM

Institutions differ in terms of what they are trying to accomplish with their undergraduate programs. Even so, there are certain hallmarks of a college-educated person. The Student Learning Imperative includes one such list:

(a) complex cognitive skills such as reflection and critical thinking;

(b) an ability to apply knowledge to practical problems encountered in one's vocation, family, or other areas of life;

(c) an understanding and appreciation of human differences;

(d) practical competence skills (e.g., decision making, conflict resolution); and

(e) a coherent, integrated constellation of personal attributes such as identity, self-esteem, confidence, integrity, aesthetic sensibilities, and civic responsibility. (American College Personnel Association 1996: 118)

Out-of-class experiences contribute to all five of these outcomes clusters. What happens beyond the classroom also directly affects student satisfaction, a key factor in persistence (Pascarella and Terenzini 1991; Tinto 1993). To illustrate, I'll briefly review some of the out-of-class experiences that are associated with three outcomes clusters: cognitive complexity, intrapersonal and interpersonal competence, practical competence (Kuh 1993).

Cognitive Complexity

The cognitive complexity domain represents skills and attitudes that enable a college-educated person to make independent judgments, think critically, and evaluate the quality of one's own thinking. The research on the influence of out-of-class experiences on cognitive development is somewhat mixed, though positive on balance (Kuh et al. 1994; Terenzini, Pascarella, and Blimling 1996). One study (Hood 1984) found no significant relationships between gains in cognitive complexity and such variables as place of residence, work experience, and participation in various campus activities. But other research shows positive relationships between out-of-class experiences and gains (Baxter Magolda 1992; Kuh 1993, 1995; Terenzini, Pascarella, and Blimling 1996).

Many of the antecedents of gains in cognitive complexity are related to peer interactions, academic-based activities such as studying, or talking with peers and faculty about academic matters or other issues related to their studies (e.g., advising, paper topics, graduate school) and leadership responsibilities. Students who are more involved than their counterparts in a range of activities (intellectual, vocational, athletic, political, social) tend to have greater cognitive development gains, variously defined (e.g., learning abstractions, applying principles, evaluating materials and methods) (Pascarella and Terenzini 1991). Living in a campus residence contributes to critical-thinking gains when the environment is conducive to such activity (Kuh et al. 1994; Pascarella, Terenzini, and Blimling 1994). That is, because gains appear to be mediated through relations with peers, the psychosocial environment of some residences (e.g., academic theme units) are more compatible with academic performance due to the characteristics of the people who live there. Work — whether on or off campus — does not seem to make a difference in terms of critical-thinking gains, at least during the first year of college (Pascarella et al. 1994).

Intrapersonal and Interpersonal Competence

Out-of-class experiences also contribute to the development of a constellation of personal attributes I call "intrapersonal and interpersonal competence" (Kuh 1993). Particularly important are activities that require high levels of commitment and engagement: performing responsibilities and managing tasks, such as leadership positions in student organizations, or being a member of an athletic team or the cast of a theatrical production, the editor or a writer on the school newspaper, or a paraprofessional such as a resident assistant or orientation leader. These involvements are highly correlated with gains in self-confidence, self-awareness, and communication skills (Kuh et al. 1994).

Certain residential experiences, such as living-learning centers, also contribute to gains in self-awareness, social competence, self-esteem, and autonomy (Blimling 1993; Kuh 1995; Pascarella et al. 1994). In large part, such gains are again a function of interpersonal environments that encourage interaction among people from different backgrounds. For example, contact with people with diverse perspectives or those who have more advanced stages of moral reasoning (e.g., discussions between first-year students and upper-class students or faculty members or staff, work-related experiences) appear to enhance moral reasoning abilities (Whiteley and Yokota 1988) and identity formation (Chickering and Reisser 1993).

Practical Competence

The practical competence outcomes cluster encompasses organizational skills associated with effective job performance preparation and personal efficacy, such as taking initiative, applied problem solving, decision making, self-management, and organizational savvy. Particularly powerful venues for gains in these areas are leadership and group or project management activities, employment, and community service (Evanoski 1988; Kuh 1995; Kuh and Lund 1994). Working on or off the campus also is important and is particularly attractive to employers (Van Horn 1995). The research is somewhat mixed, however, with regard to involvement in extracurricular activities and acquisition of practical competence. For example, some studies show that participating in co-curricular activities does not have a direct effect on career choice; others say such activities influence career selection, especially for women choosing science-related, sex-atypical careers (Kuh et al. 1994; Pascarella and Terenzini 1991).

Summary

This brief overview is necessarily incomplete and does not do justice to the rich harvest of learning that occurs outside the classroom.[1] Nonetheless, four points stand out. First, a variety of out-of-class experiences contribute to desired outcomes of college. Second, many of the gains associated with out-of-class experiences are mediated through contacts with peers and class-related assignments (e.g., studying, internships). Third, the more powerful experiences are those that demand sustained effort (e.g., planning, decision making) and require that students interact with people from different groups (e.g., faculty, administrators, trustees, employers) and peers from different backgrounds.

Finally, the impact of college is most potent when in-class and out-of-class experiences are complementary. For this reason, strategies are needed that encourage students to systematically think about what they are learning from their classes and from experiences outside the classroom and to apply what they are learning to various aspects of their lives — their studies, family and peer relations, employment, and so forth.

Implications of the Research on Out-of-Class Experiences

One immediate implication of the research is that student learning and institutional productivity can be improved by intentionally connecting in-class and out-of-class learning. There are many examples of this — academic theme residences, study abroad, community service, and internships, to name a few. But only small numbers of faculty and students are involved in one or more of these. To increase the number of complementary experiences and participants, a major structural obstacle to collaboration must be addressed:

> Higher education traditionally has organized its activities into "academic affairs" (learning, curriculum, classrooms, cognitive development) and "student affairs" (cocurriculum, student activities, residential life, affective or personal development). However, this dichotomy has little relevance to post-college life, where the quality of one's job performance, family life, and community activities are all highly dependent on cognitive and affective skills. Indeed, it is difficult to classify many important adult skills (e.g., leadership, creativity, citizenship, ethical behavior, self-understanding, teaching, mentoring) as either cognitive or affective. (American College Personnel Association 1996: 118)

Another obstacle needing attention is the differing views of faculty, student affairs professionals, and academic administrators regarding the relative worth of in-class and out-of-class activities. These groups typically attach different values to such experiences; in turn, their views determine what they spend time on and what they think is worth assessing. The differing views spring from different (and sometimes competing) assumptions about what constitutes learning and frequently short-circuit well-intentioned efforts to promote collaboration. Working with Karen Arnold, Trudy Banta, Lee Upcraft, and others, I've described these different views or mental models of what matters to student learning and personal development (Arnold and Kuh in press; Banta and Kuh 1997; Kuh et al. 1994). The short version goes like this.

Faculty tend to emphasize activities that are central to the academic program. What matters most to them in terms of student learning are the curriculum (especially the major), the material covered in the courses they teach, class-based activities, and their research insofar as it informs their work with students. Some allied institutional processes are necessary — admissions, financial aid, registration. To faculty, most of the other programs and services are nonessential; some are viewed as distractions to serious academic effort — jobs and certain social events, to name a few.

On the other hand, student affairs professionals see participation in the formal extracurriculum as essential to a well-rounded education — student government and other organizations, social events, and leadership opportunities associated with the formal extracurriculum (student government, etc.). Although classes are obviously important, student affairs professionals believe that out-of-class involvements are necessary to prepare for life after college. Support services are a sort of safety net for catching and propping up students who encounter problems that can undermine academic success.

Students and external stakeholders have their own views of what matters. Traditional-age students want to make friends and be accepted by their peers, manage newfound independence and concomitant responsibilities, and perform (reasonably) well in their classes. In contrast, older students emphasize academic performance and want their studies to be relevant to their jobs.

Faculty, student affairs staff, and other professionals who shape undergraduate learning environments typically emphasize those things over which they are expected to exert influence. In large part, the different views of faculty, staff, and students toward what matters in undergraduate education are learned. By ignoring the differences — which we are good at — relatively little meaningful cooper-

By ignoring [our] differences – which we are good at – relatively little meaningful cooperation occurs between academic and student affairs, and few intentional links are made between what students do in class with their interests and life outside the classroom.

• •

ation occurs between academic and student affairs, and few intentional links are made between what students do in class with their interests and life outside the classroom. For example, the majority of undergraduates today work, either on or off the campus, though many faculty and staff act as if this were not so; some lament it! As a result, employment is considered a distraction, rather than a bona fide learning opportunity. The trade-off is diluted intellectual and personal development.

The research on out-of-class experiences and learning is fairly clear and persuasive. Certain arrangements are more productive in fostering engagement in educationally purposeful activities that produce greater learning gains. Many of the more developmentally powerful arrangements don't cost any more than what most institutions are doing now. It was this realization that led to the Student Learning Imperative.

THE STUDENT LEARNING IMPERATIVE

The Student Learning Imperative (SLI) was commissioned by the American College Personnel Association (ACPA). It has been subsequently used at scores of institutions to guide institutional improvement efforts and tacitly endorsed by other groups, including the National Association of Student Personnel Administrators (NASPA) and AAHE. The SLI is a clarion call for colleges and universities to create the "conditions that motivate and inspire students to devote time and energy to educationally-purposeful activities" (ACPA 1994: 1). Its thesis is simple: Student affairs should be a major contributor to student

The SLI emphasizes the need for a rapprochement between academic and student affairs in order to make students' in-class and out-of-class experiences more complementary, thereby enhancing student learning.

● ●

learning by helping students connect academics with out-of-class experiences, a position advanced previously (e.g., Boyer 1987; Brown 1972; Kuh et al. 1991; National Association of Student Personnel Administrators 1987). The SLI suggests two priorities. First, student affairs must focus more of its resources and efforts on promoting learning, consistent with the institution's mission and faculty goals for student performance. Second, more collaboration is needed among faculty, academic administrators, and student life professionals to create the conditions under which students learn best.

The SLI does not and cannot stand alone. Its agenda should be considered in relation to other major statements about the undergraduate experience. The Wingspread Report (1993) in particular expresses many of the same themes, such as the need for collaboration between groups inside and outside the academy. The SLI emphasizes the need for a rapprochement between academic and student affairs in order to make students' in-class and out-of-class experiences more complementary, thereby enhancing student learning. Next, I'll describe how it was developed and some of the ways it has been used.

The History and Current Status of the SLI

With the support of the American College Personnel Association, Charles Schroeder (University of Missouri-Columbia) hosted a small group at his Estes Park, Colorado, mountain retreat in October 1993. This group included Alexander Astin, Helen Astin, Paul Bloland, K. Patricia Cross, James Hurst, Theodore Marchese, Elizabeth Nuss, Ernest Pascarella, Anne Pruitt, Michael Rooney, and

me. For three days we discussed what the research and our experience pointed to with regard to the conditions that mattered most to student learning and the ways to encourage faculty, staff, and others to work together to create these conditions. At some point I became the group's designated scribe and drafted what subsequently became the SLI.

Thanks to Schroeder (he was ACPA president at that time), student learning was the theme for ACPA's 1994 national meeting the following March. A draft of the SLI was given to all registrants, who had several opportunities to discuss the document, suggest revisions, and explore potential applications. In July 1994, the SLI was subsequently distributed to all ACPA members and the leaders of other higher education associations. Since then, much more has happened as a result of, and in response to, the SLI. In reviewing what follows, think about how your institution could use the SLI to initiate and support interventions to enhance the quality of the undergraduate experience.

● In October 1994, Bowling Green State University hosted a teleconference focused on the SLI. Several of the contributors to the SLI were there: Pat Cross, Charles Schroeder, me, and some others. The event was beamed live to about 120 sites in the United States and Canada, with an estimated 9,000 people participating. A videotape of the conference can be obtained from Bowling Green State.

● The National Association of Student Personnel Administrators — another national student affairs association, with a substantial membership base — focused its 1996 annual meeting on student learning. A new era of cooperation is under way between ACPA and NASPA, as they use the same document as a frame of reference for the professional development of their members.

● In 1996, NASPA incorporated student

learning into its mission statement. In addition, a NASPA-appointed study group is preparing a monograph to extend the applications of the ideas in the SLI; it will include papers by Karen Arnold, Marcia Baxter Magolda, Ernest Pascarella, John Schuh, Patrick Terenzini, Lee Upcraft, Elizabeth Whitt, and others.

● Several summer institutes focusing on the SLI have been held, beginning with the University of Missouri-Columbia in 1995. James Madison University attracted more than 175 participants from across the country to its oversubscribed second annual institute in 1997, including numerous faculty-staff teams. In July 1997, the annual University of Northern Colorado summer institute also examined the implications of the SLI.

● Publications have featured the SLI. Among the more prominent so far are the March 1996 special issue of the *Journal of College Student Development* and a special issue of the *College Student Affairs Journal*. Most impressive has been the emergence of a new journal, *About Campus,* a magazine devoted to encouraging collaboration among student affairs, academic affairs, and others. Modeled after *Change* magazine, *About Campus* is cosponsored by ACPA and Jossey-Bass; with a circulation of about 10,000, it is one of the most widely read higher education periodicals.

● To ensure attention to the SLI agenda in student affairs, the themes of the 1998 ACPA and NASPA conferences are, respectively, "Gateway to Learning: Promoting Student Success" and "Leadership for Learning."

● Finally, and most important, the Student Learning Imperative has spawned numerous institutional improvement efforts. Let me give you just a few examples.

Local Initiatives

In February 1997, senior academic and student affairs officers of the University of Wisconsin system met for a day and a half at the River Falls campus to focus on issues outlined in the SLI. The meeting was historic, not only because it was the first to bring together these two groups of campus leaders but also because additional collaborative activities were subsequently developed, including cooperation on a systemwide service-learning grant proposal. In June 1997, the senior student affairs officers of the SUNY system devoted their annual summer retreat to examining the implications of the SLI; in the coming year, they plan to work with their academic affairs counterparts on the SLI agenda.

In April 1997, the University of Georgia (UGA) held its annual faculty symposium in the north Georgia mountains. The theme for this event, "Enhancing the Undergraduate Experience," was suggested in the 1996 state of the university address by the then UGA president, Charles Knapp, who drew substantially from the SLI in declaring that enhancing the quality of the undergraduate experience at UGA simply had to be the top priority of the institution during the coming years. For the first time, student affairs staff helped plan and participate in what had been previously a retreat exclusive to faculty and academic administrators. Similar symposia and workshops have been held at the University of Connecticut, University of Delaware, SUNY at Brockport, Hamline University, Ithaca College, and other institutions.

The SLI is not targeted primarily to residential campuses. Two-year colleges and large, urban universities also are resonating to its message. Monroe Community College in Rochester, New York, focused a daylong symposium on the SLI and, much to its surprise, attracted more than 150 participants from nearby institutions, twice the expected number! Sinclair Community College in Ohio and Maricopa Community College in Arizona are planning similar symposia next fall. Portland

State University, Kennesaw State University, and the Indianapolis campus of Indiana University (IUPUI) are other examples of how the SLI has found its way into institutional improvement efforts.

At Portland State, student affairs staff are team-teaching with faculty in their nationally recognized Freshman Inquiry Program. This program ensures a small class (twenty to twenty-five students) for most first-year students. As a result, faculty discovered that they were getting to know students extremely well in these classes, much better than they were prepared to know them! Students introduced personal and career-oriented issues during advising sessions and class discussions that faculty were not prepared to handle. Several student affairs professionals were already involved in Freshman Inquiry, and their expertise proved so valuable that student affairs staff members are now helping to plan and teach Freshman Inquiry. City Quest is Portland State's orientation program; linked to Freshman Inquiry, City Quest is a model for how orientation can be an educationally powerful blend of academic and social experiences. PSU has also created a position jointly funded by University College and Student Affairs for someone to team-teach in the Freshman Inquiry Program and to promote additional collaborative activities between academic and student affairs.

All this is to show that there is fairly broad interest in the SLI agenda on the part of faculty, academic administrators, and student affairs. My experience on more than two dozen campuses during this time is that faculty are as enthusiastic as the student affairs professionals are about the benefits of potential collaboration. Why such interest?

To paraphrase Woody Allen, timing is everything. A discernable shift is under way toward focusing institutional effort on undergraduate education, a trend more than a decade in the making (Barr and Tagg 1995). In addition, the SLI outlines a much-needed shared vision of what matters to undergradu-

ate learning by emphasizing the importance of intentionally connecting out-of-class experiences to the learning enterprise. It specifically challenges student affairs to become a partner with faculty and academic affairs in institutional improvement efforts, thus capitalizing on the knowledge that collaboration is essential in an increasingly complicated world.

REALIZING THE PROMISE OF SEAMLESS LEARNING

A key task in any effort to enhance the quality of the undergraduate experience is to become familiar with promising practices and to intentionally arrange mutually supportive in-class and out-of-class learning experiences. One way to start is to substitute activities and programs that the research shows work well for things that don't. Many of the things that work well require collaboration if they are to be effective.

For example, having students participate in learning communities — that is, co-enrolling new students in two to three courses — is more effective than their taking classes that are not linked intellectually or socially. A powerful variation for residential campuses is to assign co-enrolled students to the same living unit, thereby creating 24-hour-a-day learning communities! Students learn more, in part because they take a seminar that helps them see the relationships among concepts from their different courses. The peer group is transformed from what is primarily a social experience to one mediated by common intellectual tasks, which leads to conversations among friends on class-related topics. Students tend to perform better academically and are more likely to stay in school. Even though such arrangements have mostly desirable effects, only a fraction of students on residential campuses are given this or a comparable option such as residences based on academic themes. To bring these learning environments online requires collaboration among — at a minimum — admissions, registrar, residence hall staff, academic administrators, and faculty. Because it can't be done any other way, the "functional silos" and "mine shafts" that have characterized colleges and universities for so long are being replaced by cross-functional teams made up of people who are forced to work together.

When students join fraternities and sororities as soon as they get to college, numerous undesirable institutional and individual student effects frequently accrue (Kuh and Arnold 1993; Pascarella et al. 1996b; Wechsler, Kuh, and Davenport 1996). Even so, only a few institutions have taken the difficult steps to defer new member recruitment to the second year. On many campuses, this is essentially a student affairs agenda. But — and this is a huge "but" — student affairs cannot change the campus culture without the support of academic administrators and faculty, clamoring for and endorsing the change, because trustees — among others — have to be convinced of its merits.

Work experience makes valuable contributions to practical competence and is viewed by employers as among the most desirable qualities a student can offer, yet many faculty and student affairs professionals ignore the potential influence of work on learning in the curriculum, individual course assignments, advising, and assessment programs.

Academic and student affairs divisions organized independent of each other are viewed by faculty, student affairs professionals, and students to be separate and often alienated from the core purposes of the institution, yet too many senior student affairs officers, provosts, and presidents seem to be satisfied with this arrangement; many even prefer it, which in itself is cause for concern.

Out-of-class experiences make important contributions to institutional goals and student learning (Astin 1993; Kuh et al. 1994; Pascarella and Terenzini 1991), yet too many provosts, academic deans, faculty leaders, and assessment team members are unaware of these contributions or cannot articulate them

Out-of-class experiences affect students in myriad ways. Some experiences complement the academic program, some compete with it, only a few are irrelevant.

• •

in a persuasive manner.

Many institutions lack evidence of the impact of out-of-class experiences on student learning, yet faculty and student affairs professionals do not often work together to develop assessment approaches, collect data, and interpret the findings with an eye toward changing institutional policies and practices to enhance student learning.

The 1997 AAHE Conference on Assessment & Quality is featuring more than twenty sessions addressing these and related assessment and institutional improvement topics. The majority of these sessions fall into four categories: (a) encouraging cross-functional collaboration (faculty, student affairs, academic affairs) on assessment and quality initiatives; (b) connecting in-class/academic goals with out-of-class experiences; (c) assessing the influence of the larger institutional environment or campus culture on out-of-class experiences and student learning; and (d) documenting the contributions of student affairs to student learning and the institutional improvement agenda. Review the abstracts from these sessions. Then, contact the presenters for additional information that may be relevant to your institutional context and your assessment and quality-improvement priorities.

CONCLUSION

Out-of-class experiences affect students in myriad ways. Some experiences complement the academic program, some compete with it, only a few are irrelevant. The Student Learning Imperative is consistent with calls that faculty, student affairs professionals, and academic administrators join together and arrange learning opportunities that help students connect what they often perceive to be disjointed, independent experiences. The result can approximate a seamless learning environment where students learn how to synthesize and integrate material introduced in the formal academic program; apply their knowledge and skills; and develop more sophisticated, thoughtful views on personal, academic, and other matters. The numerous assessment and institutional improvement tasks that flow from this agenda not only warrant our attention but are essential if higher education is to meet the expectations of its various stakeholders. ◆

Note

[1]This summary of the contributions of out-of-class experiences to desired college outcomes draws substantially from my ASHE-ERIC monograph *Student Learning Outside the Classroom* (Kuh et al. 1994). Out-of-class experiences also contribute to the domains not reviewed in this paper, such as knowledge acquisition/application and humanitarianism. The effects on knowledge acquisition seem to be mediated primarily through class-related activities such as studying and internships. Students report the fewest gains in knowledge application, though out-of-class activities and opportunities are potentially rich for such applications; employment and community are just two areas that offer ample opportunities.

REFERENCES

American College Personnel Association. *The Student Learning Imperative.* Washington, DC: ACPA, 1994. [Reprinted in the March 1996 *Journal of College Student Development,* vol. 37, pp. 118-22.]

Arnold, K. A., and G. D. Kuh. "What Matters in Undergraduate Education? Mental Models, Student Learning, and Student Affairs." *Student Affairs and Student Learning,* edited by E. J. Whitt. Washington, DC: NASPA, in press.

Astin, A. W. *What Matters in College: Four Critical Years Revisited.* San Francisco: Jossey-Bass, 1993.

Banta, T.W., and G. D. Kuh. "A Missing Link in Assessment: Collaboration Between Academic and Student Affairs." Paper presented at the AAHE Conference on Assessment & Quality, Miami, June 1997.

Barr, R.B., and J. Tagg. "From Teaching to Learning — A New Paradigm for Undergraduate Education." *Change* 27 (November/December 1995): 13-25.

Baxter Magolda, M. *Knowing and Reasoning in College: Gender Related Patterns in Students' Intellectual Development.* San Francisco: Jossey-Bass, 1992.

———. "Promoting Intellectual Development Through the Co-Curriculum." Paper presented at the meeting of the Association for the Study of Higher Education, Tucson, November 1994.

Blimling, G. "The Influence of College Residence Halls on Students." *Higher Education: Handbook of Theory and Research.* Vol. 9, edited by J. Smart, pp. 248-307. New York: Agathon, 1993.

Boyer, E. *College: The Undergraduate Experience in America.* New York: Harper, 1987.

Brown, R. D. *Tomorrow's Higher Education: A Return to the Academy.* Washington, DC: ACPA, 1972.

Bruffee, K. A. *Collaborative Learning: Higher Education, Interdependence, and the Authority of Knowledge.* Baltimore: Johns Hopkins University Press, 1993.

Chickering, A. W., and L. Reisser. *Education and Identity.* Rev. ed. San Francisco: Jossey-Bass, 1993.

Evanoski, P. "An Assessment of the Impact of Helping on the Helper for College Students." *College Student Journal* 22 (1988): 2-6.

Ewell, P. T. "Restoring Our Links With Society: The Neglected Art of Collective Responsibility." *Metropolitan Universities* vol. 5, no. 1 (1994): 79-87.

Hood, A. B. "Student Development: Does Participation Affect Growth?" *Bulletin of the Association of College Unions International* 54 (1984): 16-19.

Kuh, G. D. "Guiding Principles for Creating Seamless Learning Environments for Undergraduates." *Journal of College Student Development* 37 (1996): 135-48.

————. "The Other Curriculum: Out-of-Class Experiences Associated With Student Learning and Personal Development." *Journal of Higher Education* 66 (1995): 123-55.

————. "In Their Own Words: What Students Learn Outside the Classroom." *American Educational Research Journal* 30 (1993): 277-304.

————, and J. A. Arnold. "Liquid Bonding: A Cultural Analysis of the Role of Alcohol in Fraternity Pledgeship." *Journal of College Student Development* 34 (1993): 327-34.

Kuh, G.D., K. B. Douglas, J. P. Lund, and J. Ramin-Gyurnek. *Student Learning Outside the Classroom: Transcending Artificial Boundaries.* ASHE-ERIC Higher Education Report, no. 8. Washington, DC: George Washington University, School of Education and Human Development, 1994.

Kuh, G. D., and J. Lund. "What Students Gain From Participating in Student Government." *Developing Student Government Leadership.* New Directions for Student Services, no. 66, edited by M. Terrell and M. Cuyjet. San Francisco:

Jossey-Bass, 1994.

Kuh, G. D., J. S. Schuh, E. J. Whitt, and Associates. *Involving Colleges: Successful Approaches to Fostering Student Learning and Personal Development Outside the Classroom.* San Francisco: Jossey-Bass, 1991.

Kuh, G. D., N. Vesper, M. R. Connolly, and C. R. Pace. (1997). *College Student Experiences Questionnaire: Revised Norms for the Third Edition.* Bloomington: Indiana University, Center for Postsecondary Research and Planning, 1997.

National Association of Student Personnel Administrators. *A Perspective on Student Affairs.* Washington, DC: NASPA, 1987.

Pace, C. R. *The Undergraduates: A Report of Their Activities and Progress in College in the 1980s.* Los Angeles: University of California-Los Angeles, Center for the Study of Evaluation, 1990.

Pascarella, E. T. "College Environmental Influences on Learning and Cognitive Development: A Critical Review and Synthesis." *Higher Education: Handbook of Theory and Research,* Vol. 1, edited by J. Smart, pp. 1-62. New York: Agathon, 1985.

————, L. Bohr, A. Nora, M. Desler, and B. Zusman. "Impacts of On-Campus and Off-Campus Work on First-Year Cognitive Outcomes." *Journal of College Student Development* 35, no. 5 (September 1994): 364-70.

Pascarella, E. T., M. Edison, A. Nora, and P. T. Terenzini. "Influences on Students' Openness to Diversity and Challenge in the First Year of College." *Journal of Higher Education* 67 (1996a): 174-95.

Pascarella, E. T., M. Edison, E. Whitt, A. Nora, L. Hagedorn, and P. T. Terenzini. (1996b).

"Cognitive Effects of Greek Affiliation During the First Year of College." *NASPA Journal* 33 (1996): 242-59.

Pascarella, E. T., and P. T. Terenzini. *How College Affects Students: Findings and Insights From Twenty Years of Research.* San Francisco: Jossey-Bass, 1991.

———— , and G. S. Blimling "The Impact of Residential Life on Students." In *Realizing the Educational Potential of Residence Halls,* edited by C. Schroeder and P. Mable, pp. 22-52. San Francisco: Jossey-Bass, 1994.

Pascarella, E. T., E. Whitt, A. Nora, M. Edison, L. Hagedorn, and P. T. Terenzini. "What Have We Learned From the First Year of the National Study of Student Learning?" *Journal of College Student Development* 37 (1996): 182-92.

Springer, L., B. Palmer, P. T. Terenzini, E. T. Pascarella, and A. Nora. "Attitudes Toward Diversity: Participation in a Racial or Cultural Awareness Workshop." *Review of Higher Education* 20, no. 1 (Fall 1996).

Springer, L., P. T. Terenzini, E. T. Pascarella, and A. Nora. "Influences on College Students' Orientations Toward Learning for Self-Understanding." *Journal of College Student Development* 36 (1995): 5-18.

Terenzini, P. T., E. T. Pascarella, and G. S. Blimling. "Students' Out-of-Class Experiences and Their Influence on Learning and Cognitive Development: A Literature Review." *Journal of College Student Development* 37 (1996): 149-62.

Terenzini, P. T., L. Springer, E. T. Pascarella, and A. Nora. "Academic and Out-of-Class Influences Affecting the Development of Students' Intellectual Orientations." *Review of Higher Education* 19 (1995a): 23-44.

———— . "Influences Affecting the Development of Students' Critical Thinking Skills." *Research in Higher Education* 36 (1995b): 23-39.

Tinto, V. *Leaving College: Rethinking the Causes and Cures of Student Attrition.* 2nd ed. Chicago: University of Chicago Press, 1993.

Van Horn, C. E. *Enhancing the Connection Between Higher Education and the Workplace: A Survey of Employers.* Denver: Education Commission of the States, 1995.

Wechsler, H., G. D. Kuh, and A. Davenport. "Fraternities, Sororities, and Binge Drinking: Results From a National Study of American Colleges." *NASPA Journal* 33 (1996): 260-79.

Whiteley, J., and N. Yokota. *The Freshman Year Experience: Character Development in the Freshman Year and Over Four Years of Undergraduate Study.* Columbia: University of South Carolina at Columbia, Center for the Study of the Freshman Year Experience, 1988.

Wingspread Group on Higher Education. *An American Imperative: Higher Expectations for Higher Education.* Racine, WI: Johnson Foundation, 1993.

George Kuh is professor of education at Indiana University Bloomington, W.W. Wright Education Building, 201 N. Rose Avenue, #4228, Bloomington, IN 47405, kuh@indiana.edu.

I remember vividly that January day, more than 20 years ago, when I was sitting in my faculty office and in walked the chair of the Sociology Department.

"Ted," she asked, "when you were in college, did you take coursework in sociology?"

"Well, no," I said, "I was an English major."

"Well," she said, "maybe as a graduate stu-

The New Conversations About Learning

Insights From Neuroscience and Anthropology, Cognitive Science and Work-Place Studies

BY THEODORE J. MARCHESE

dent, you took courses in research?"

"Oh yes," I said. "All of us at Michigan had to do a research sequence."

"Well," she said, "one for two may be close enough. I just got a phone call from our colleague who teaches the required statistics course for sociology majors and she'll have to take a medical leave this spring. Could you stand in and teach that course for us?"

Through a hurried sequence of events, ten days later I stood in front of that class, supposedly ready to teach statistics. I was, at the time, nothing if not conscientious; I read all the textbooks and chose what I thought was a good one, prepared a careful syllabus, and worked hard on my lectures. During the semester, I think I can say, I was respectful toward students; I tried to get everybody

involved; I kept my office hours; I got the homework back on time; we covered every chapter; my tests were tough but fair.

That summer, two or three weeks after the end of the semester, I remember the department head again coming into my office and this time saying, "Ted, you must be an excellent teacher!"

"How's that?" I asked.

"Well," she said, "the computer center just sent me a printout of all the student evaluations for the department's courses and your course had a 4.7 on a 5-point scale . . . the second-highest mark of any course in the whole department!"

And I can hear her again — it was music to my young ears! — saying, "Ted, you must be an excellent teacher."

In making choices about what to teach and how to assess it, clarity about the character of learning we intend for students must be an essential bedrock for what we do.

● ●

Reflecting back on that experience, I'd have to tell you now that of the 28 students in that class, all but two passed the exams, but maybe only half of them ever really got it. If you gave them all my final exam six months later, perhaps three of them would have passed. It turns out that the next course they took in their department's sequence was one on research methods; but the person who taught that focused on qualitative research and field-based studies, so none of the parametric statistics I taught came to be practiced or applied. If you ask me now about "quantitative reasoning" or "statistical literacy" as possible outcomes, the answer is, 20 years ago I'd never heard of those things.

What these students were good at — and I played right into this — was feeding back correct answers; they had mastered the arts of short-term memory and recall. The whole class was a wonderful example of what the British call "surface learning." But very little "deep learning" — which comes with time, depth, practice, and reinforcement — seems in retrospect to have occurred.

So I return to the question, Is Ted an excellent teacher? Today, were I up for promotion, I could put together one heck of a portfolio based on that course. I'd have, first of all, letters from students saying how much they enjoyed my course. I'd have a letter from my chair, who'd vouch again, Ted is an excellent teacher. And I'd have that big 4.7, an irrefutable number.

Today I have doubts, as you sense, about whether I did right by those students. But this is my point: I don't think you can answer the question — Is Ted an excellent teacher? — without having an idea about the kind of learning that was appropriate from that course. If surface learning (and student satis-

faction) will do, the answer might well be "yes"; if a different, deeper character of learning were supposed to occur, then "no."

This insight is the starting premise of my presentation. That is, in making judgments about programs or curricula, about teaching or teachers, the ideas we hold about learning itself will and should be decisive. In making choices about what to teach and how to assess it, clarity about the character of learning we intend for students must be an essential bedrock for what we do.

To take an assessment example, should we use a standardized instrument or short-item questionnaire to find out about our students' learning? Or should we put our chips behind direct faculty readings of student work? Are the forms of "authentic assessment" that Grant Wiggins urges upon us . . . portfolios and the like . . . worth the time and effort? In fact, there's a case to be made for each of these options. But, again, you can't answer questions such as these without being clear about learning itself, and then without consequent ideas about the role of assessment in revealing and prompting such learning.

My intention here, then, is to talk about what usually gets left out — learning itself — as a way of helping you think about the choices you make in enacting and assessing undergraduate education. What I propose to do might be thought of as a little tour de terrain, an all-too-brief look at a whole string of conversations about learning that are going forward today across several disciplines.

There is high danger in such an ambition; you will immediately know that I am not a member of most of these disciplines. I am a writer, editor, and sometime teacher. What I'm attempting to provide is a selective, user's-end view of intriguing research, without claiming expertise in any of the things I'm about to report.

Indeed, if I might paraphrase J.L. Austin's famous remark about philosophers for my own role here, I'd say of any oversimplification that follows, "One might be tempted to call it the occupational disease of keynoters, if it were not their occupation."

THE TEACHER'S WISDOM

For most of our professional lives, we've had two ways of knowing about learning.

The first is through a wisdom literature, in which famous teachers tell us how to instruct students. This literature is as old as written history itself. To take three examples, a traditional Chinese proverb tells us, "Teachers open the door. You enter by yourself." Aristotle echoed this when he said, "What we have to learn to do, we learn by doing." Galileo admonished that "You cannot teach a man anything; you can only help him find it within himself."

Reading admonitions like these, you wonder whether 20th-century social science has busied itself proving what's already known.

There's a related but more rigorous literature, of course, in philosophy, about knowledge and knowing, to which I'll return. Here let me add a particular insight from ancient Greece, attributed to Aristotle, namely that there is a difference between knowledge, understanding, and wisdom. If knowledge implies basic comprehension, understanding means comprehending well enough to be able to *do* the thing, and wisdom reflects dispositions to act wisely.

Two years ago at this AAHE Conference on Assessment & Quality, the systems theorist Russell Ackoff spread knowledge, understanding, and wisdom across a spectrum, and to the left of them data and information. His point was that ever so much of what transpires in undergraduate education today has to do with the left and middle portions of that spectrum — with data, information, and knowledge — and that the goal of reform ought to be to move the locus of attention further to the right, toward greater emphasis on understanding and wisdom . . . a point I take as wise.

Wisdom literatures have brought us important insight over the years. Who thought more deeply about teaching and learning than Alfred North Whitehead? I reread his short book *The Aims of Education,* published in 1929, every two or three years. I think also of the wonderful books on teaching from Gilbert Highet and Kenneth Eble. And, good as any of these, Parker Palmer's *The Courage to Teach,* due later this year.

PSYCHOLOGICAL STUDIES

In the present century, psychologists have developed a huge literature on learning. Over these years, psychology has been dominated by behaviorist models, then developmental ones — think of Thorndike, Skinner, and Piaget; more lately it has been cognitive and constructivist (led often by Jerome Bruner). Sadly, perhaps, psychologists and their social science kinfolk have been dismissive of thinkers working from wisdom or humanistic traditions; but they, in turn, are marginalized by humanists (as reductionist) and by "hard" scientists (as "soft"). And when it comes to the practice side of psychological research — educational research — then, I'm afraid, we're into true dismissiveness.

All of which is unfortunate in that it can brush aside important insight. There are indeed good reasons not to get carried away with the corpus of ed-psych research, not least because it has too often been theory-free, consumed by measurement, and in love with the trivial. A more important thing to note may be this: Often what it has to say about teaching is based on quite thin ideas about learning itself . . . witness all the studies that took student performance on final exams as the outcome criterion.

Having said this much, now let me say that cognitive psychologists — in psych departments and ed schools alike — have achieved understandings over the decades that meet high tests of rigor and generalizability, and that all who teach must heed. Who among us can doubt the importance to learning of feedback and reflection? Of intrinsic motivation? Or doubt the difficulty of teaching for transfer?

One of the most important findings from cognitive psychology surely has been the whole matter of prior beliefs and mental models; let me focus here on that one finding. The insight is simple enough: It begins with the innate need of humans to make meaning out of their experience of the world. So we develop, at quite early ages — as five-year-olds, for example — basic sets of ideas about how the world works, what's dangerous, who's friendly, about right and wrong, what to like and how to behave, and so on. The scary part is that these childhood versions of reality tend to get pretty hard-wired into the brain and prove quite resistant to change: Once we think we've figured out some corner of the world, we tend to see what we want to see and hear what we want to hear, bending subsequent experience into confirmation. I say "scary" because the existence of prior beliefs can be a major impediment to subsequent learning: The beliefs, after all, may be objectively wrong, or bigoted, or dysfunctional, and block fair and open encounter with the new or different. Very significantly, prior beliefs turn out to be especially impervious to classroom-based instruction, and especially to teaching as telling.

There's a chilling example of this in a video made at Harvard several years ago, called *A Private Universe*. The heart of it consists of interviews of Harvard graduates on the day of graduation. Picture the Harvard Yard, gowns and bands, proud parents with cameras, and a wandering interviewer asking the new graduates a seemingly simple question: Why is it warmer in summer than in winter?

Our graduates are nothing if not confident. "Well," they say, "let's see, in summertime the Sun comes a lot closer to the Earth and, well, you know, the closer it gets the more heat you're going to have . . . right?" Now, mind you, these are students who've taken units on the solar system back in junior high school, who've had three years of high school science, who took physics and/or astronomy at Har-

vard, and who probably got an "A" in them every time out. Yet they persist in a pre-Copernican view of how the world works. The point of the video is to show how mental models, once formed, are incredibly resistant to change, especially from conventional instruction.

A larger-scale example of this appears this fall in an *American Journal of Physics* article by Indiana University physicist Richard Hake. It looks at the impacts of instruction on student beliefs across some 62 first-level physics courses, 6,549 students in all, from rural high schools through Ivy universities. At the start and finish of each of these courses, students were administered an instrument called the Force Concept Inventory, a well-developed diagnostic instrument that assesses student orientation toward mechanics . . . it basically looks to see whether people's view of mechanics — of how the physical world works — is pre-Newtonian or post-Newtonian.

Many of us, like the students in the 62 courses, tend to carry in our heads naive, commonsensical ideas about mechanics that are pre-Newtonian. Wrong as they may be, these views turn out to be ever so resistant to change by conventional instruction. What the study shows is that in traditional physics courses — lecture-based, recipe labs, right-answer quizzes and tests — the impacts on deeper beliefs about the physical world are small . . . about .22 on the instrument's measurement scale. Strikingly, the small-impacts finding held whether the instructor was an experienced "teacher of the year," a brand-new instructor, or anything in-between. Gravity, light, motion, feather vs. pellet in a vacuum, whatever these students believed beforehand was pretty much what they believed at the end . . . notwithstanding all the right answers they produced for exams.

Hake's study is compelling because his set of 62 courses included 41 that were taught in quite a different way, emphasizing more active forms of learning ("heads-on"), problem-based labs ("hands-on"), and immediate feedback through discussion with peers and/or instructors. On the same assessment scale, the gain among students was on the order of .52 — quite a striking difference, though still a less-than-full victory in terms of changing mental models, which (again) remain ever-so-tough to alter. The good news here, of course, is that smart instruction does work . . . the unhappy thought is that such approaches are hardly yet the norm.

I want to conclude these remarks on wisdom literatures and cognitive psychology by pointing out that both have historically been focused on the *teacher*, not on learning itself. Even in classic experimental designs — where you set up a treatment, the teacher teaches a certain way (as in Hake's courses), then you observe student performance as the outcome — you're basically treating the mind as a black box. At best, the method allows for inference about what's happening in student brains . . . potentially valuable, as when we infer the operation of mental models, but an inference all the same.

THE NEUROSCIENCES

What's new this decade is the emergence of a robust, exploding set of literatures in the neurosciences. I use the plural here because brain research now attracts the attention of scientists from at least half a dozen specialties: neurophysiologists, molecular biologists, neuroanatomists, certain chemists and medical researchers, and so on. The big breakthrough, especially this decade, has been the availability of PET scan and functional MRI devices that allow scientists to observe mental activity directly, to take a "picture" of the brain at work. So exciting are the possibilities here that there's been an outpouring of federal funding in support of neuroscientific inquiry. It is the "Decade of the Brain."

With this activity, a veritable flood of discoveries has come forward on the functioning of the brain. These have excited hopes among educators that soon, at last, we'll learn what

No scientist has yet come up with a coherent set of ideas about how the brain works that would be persuasive and usable for those of us who teach.

• •

really happens inside all those student heads and have a scientific basis for teaching.

But, alas, not yet . . . and maybe not soon. When you get neuroscientists together in a room with educators, one of the first things you learn is that there have been a tremendous number of findings, yes, but the meaning of many of them remains in dispute. Another circumstance is that for all the findings, there's precious little theory to connect or interpret them . . . and there's nothing so useful as a good theory, Kurt Lewin taught us. No scientist has yet come up with a coherent set of ideas about how the brain works that would be persuasive and usable for those of us who teach.

For the past 18 months I've been a participant in a series of Wingspread conversations sponsored by John Abbott's 21st Century Learning Initiative, which has brought together scientists with educators to try to make sense out of these new literatures. One of the things that I've observed at these meetings, and that I'm glad for, is that neuroscientists are reluctant to generalize from the findings they have so far, to tell us as teachers what we should be doing.

One reason for this is that much of the brain research that's gone on has been done as an aspect of larger projects on the "high-dollar diseases" . . . studies of brain functioning among Alzheimer's patients, for example, or alcoholics; these aren't studies of college sophomores. And, thankfully, good scientists are reluctant to make prescriptive leaps from Alzheimer's to college classrooms.

An interesting thing to me is that the more you get to know the newer brain literatures, how few surprises there are. So many of the findings seem to confirm what we've already known, or at least theorized.

To the neuroscientist, learning is a whole-person/
whole-brain activity that confounds received categorizations.
● ●

To take one tiny example, if I look out the window and see a tree, our commonsense idea about what's happening is that a picture of the tree comes in through the retina and an image of it forms straightaway on some screen inside our head, just like photography. Well, of course, it doesn't quite work that way . . . there is no "screen" and, more importantly, the mind's image of that tree is far from a simple reproduction of an external reality: 80 percent of what winds up in the brain's image comes from information, ideas, and feelings that are already in the brain, just 20 percent from outside. The learning here is that when we look at a tree, or another person, or hear an idea, the sense we form of it is highly colored by a whole range of prior experiences and emotional dispositions. What we have from the brain researchers, then, seems just to confirm what we knew before about the power of the mental models we carry around in our head.

The University of Oregon's Robert Sylwester argues that we shouldn't be so surprised when neuroscientific findings parallel what we've found as teachers or educational researchers. If I have 28 students in my statistics class, I have a semester-long opportunity to observe 28 brains in operation . . . the inferences I'd draw just from watching what works with them reflect a form of "brain research." It may not be science and it does have its limits, but there's a "wisdom of practice" teachers develop that warrants respect.

None of this is to say, however, that there's nothing new coming out of the neurosciences. I'll present a few summary findings next. Here I want to note that brain science provides us with new ways — and vocabularies — for talking about learning. As educators, for example, we've long spoken about how student development in college is a function of the intellec-

tual and affective . . . but these "domains" of an earlier psychology are not the way neuroscientists describe things. They pay little heed, too, to the nice distinctions we educators want to make between younger, college-age, and adult learners, or to our preoccupation with "learning styles"; I've not found one of them who thinks of "intelligence" as a unitary, fixed characteristic of individuals, or who thinks of the brain as an "empty vessel" or computer-like machine. To the neuroscientist, learning is a whole-person/whole-brain activity that confounds received categorizations.

COGNITIVE SCIENCE

Right alongside the neurosciences, new, hybrid forms of cognitive science have emerged. Lacking a tidy definition, let me proceed with an example, albeit one that conflates a string of actual experiments.

Imagine an experiment in which rats are being raised in a series of five boxes. In the first box, you have a single rat, raised the usual (sterile) way. In box two, you have a rat raised the same way, except that it is given toys to play with. In box three, same idea, except that the rat's toys are changed every week. Box four, same idea, changed toys, but there are several rats growing up together. In box five, you have several rats, rich toys, but each rat is removed from the cage every day and lovingly stroked for 15 minutes. At the end of a time period, all these rats are given learning tasks to accomplish: pushing levers for food, finding their way through mazes, and so on. The finding, when you look at their respective abilities to learn these tasks, is a learning curve that goes up steadily from the first box through the fifth . . . a 25 percent gain in "rat intelligence," if you will, attributable to differences of upbringing. The new cognitive scientists buttress these observations by measurements of brain weight and cortical development in the different rats, and with counts of cells and synapses. What we have in today's cognitive sciences, then, is a new blend of psychology and biology.

At this point you might be thinking, well, we're still talking rats, not students; but it would be hard to get your university's human-subjects committee to approve an experiment that requisitioned sophomore brains for counting and weighing. On the other hand, rats and humans have about 95 percent of their genetic material in common. The real news in these experiments is not just the importance of rich, social environments and of nurture in upbringing but the brain's *plasticity,* its ability to realize new capacities in response to experience. Again, none of the neuroscientists I speak with thinks of "intelligence" as an innate capacity fixed at birth. Indeed, the best news (at least for adults my age!) is the evidence coming forth of the brain's plasticity across the lifespan, of human abilities ever to learn, to "effloresce" in creativity in the right conditions of challenge and safety. Early experiences and genetic inheritance are very important; yet all kinds of people are capable of incredible feats of learning through decades of their life. Just how "new" an understanding we should think this is I'm not so sure; but it is a valuable counter to our academic folk wisdom that wants to categorize people early and keep them there.

In the Wingspread meetings I mentioned earlier, there have been a few (brave) souls willing to help construct summary lists of learnings from the neuro- and cognitive sciences; let me share two such here in abridged form.

The first is from Dee Dickinson, head of Seattle's New Horizons for Learning project, and is based on the work of Marian Diamond of UC-Berkeley. Four of Dickinson's items in summary form are:
- the brain is remarkably plastic across the lifespan;
- powerful learning is prompted when all five senses are engaged;
- adequate time is needed for each phase of information processing (input/assimilation/output); and

- emotional well-being is essential to intellectual functioning, indeed to survival.

Little on this list comes as a surprise. Experiments with the teaching of language, for example, have shown how quickly and lastingly a new tongue is learned when students can hear, live, speak, act, and sing it. Good teachers have always known that speed in producing answers isn't a good indicator of inherent capacity in students. And readers of Daniel Goleman's recent book, *Emotional Intelligence,* know well the cortex's ties to a powerful limbic system and the social-emotional origins of thinking.

Here is a second list, this one by Geoffrey Caine, an Australian living in San Diego . . . he and his wife, Renate Caine, have made a specialty of translating these literatures for K-12 educators:
- body, mind, and brain exist in dynamic unity;
- our brain is a social brain;
- the search for meaning is innate;
- the brain establishes meaning through patterning;
- emotions are crucial to patterning;
- learning involves conscious and unconscious processes;
- complex learning is enhanced by challenge, inhibited by threat; and
- every brain is uniquely organized, with resulting differences of talent and preference.

One of the things scientists have established pretty clearly is stated next to last on this list: When humans confront a situation they perceive as threatening, their brain "downshifts" . . . higher-order cortical functioning is supplanted by the more elemental limbic . . . the emotions come to rule. The point to ponder — the Caines make it — is the high reliance in American classrooms on sticks and carrots, on competition and scarce rewards, an ethos that can engender a mix of student attitudes somewhere between grudging compliance and sullen disengagement. High challenge, yes, they say; high anxiety, no.

EVOLUTIONARY STUDIES

My next disciplinary excursion is into the companion fields of evolutionary biology and evolutionary psychology, the latter often associated with the more recent work of Jerome Bruner. There was a wonderful review of Bruner's latest book (questions and all) by Clifford Geertz in the *New York Review* earlier this spring. Also this spring, Stephen Jay Gould, as you may have seen in the *New Yorker*, attacked evolutionary biology as an immature, overreaching form of science, as sociobiology in new clothes.

So these fields are not without controversy. But I take the "finding" that follows as at least provocative. It is that natural dispositions and ways of knowing can be identified in the human species, approaches to learning that proved evolutionarily successful over the ages and are all but in our gene pool. In effect, there's a "natural" way of learning for humans. What is it? you say, surely with interest. The answer: apprenticeship.

How the evolutionists get there is by looking back at how humans learned over the course of the 1,000 or so generations of knowable (recorded) history. All prior societies, for example, have had the very problem we confront today, that of how to bring young people up into valued adult roles. The approach of a whole range of societies, across a tremendous number of generations, was apprenticeship. The way people became midwives, stonecutters, artists, shamans, masons, hunters, a hundred other occupations, was through socially organized apprenticeships. That was true right up until the 1840s in England and until the Civil War in the United States, when universal schooling became the new way of preparing young people for adult roles. It's only in the last six generations or so in the industrial democracies that we've had formal mechanisms of schooling. But for the figurative 994 generations that came before, young people learned what they learned through apprenticeship.

Another way to confirm this observation is through anthropological studies that look cross-culturally at how societies today that do not have universal schooling prepare their young; again the answer is through forms of apprenticeship. Studies have been done, for example, of how girls or young women become midwives in rural Yucatan or Zimbabwe; they learn that role by attaching themselves to experienced practitioners.

As Jean Lave outlined in her 1991 book *Situated Learning*, there are many forms of apprenticeship across time, occupations, and cultures, yet commonalities, too. These common elements came to be fleshed out in a flurry of literature that appeared in the early 1990s. Apprenticeship has typically been a cohort activity. That is, there were often two or three masters and a whole set of apprentices, rather than simply a one-to-one arrangement. The master was both taskmaster and mentor. Among the masters and apprentices there was always rich conversation about what it is they were learning . . . the important knowledge was tacit, seldom written down, and had to be learned by doing and talking. Very importantly, too, care was taken that the young person always understood the context, the real-life meaning of each lesson or step . . . the classic example is from stonecutting, where the apprentice knew the stone had to be absolutely square to fit just so in the wall of the cathedral.

Finally, there was a notion in apprenticeship that today's scholars call "scaffolding." The idea here is that in the earliest years of apprenticeship, the tasks were highly structured and supervised. But gradually that oversight and support were removed, so that by the time the apprentice was an adult — which in most societies meant age 16 — he or she would be able to do it alone and be free-standing in the trade or craft. The young adult would be, in today's expression, an independent learner.

Interest in apprenticeship has been keen in the K-12 reform conversation in this country. One of the things people notice, when they look at that model, is how utterly teacher-dependent American education has become. Even at the college level, you and I might notice, we have an almost entirely teacher-driven system. We preach the goal of preparing independent learners, but you can go to any college bookstore and watch yourself as second-semester seniors file through to buy their assigned texts and notepads for the prepackaged courses they'll take.

SITUATED LEARNING

Our next set of literatures — closely related in their findings to the evolutionary studies we've just discussed — derive from workplace studies. These have been essentially ethnographic inquiries into questions such as, How do new employees enter a work setting and learn to contribute? What does it take to become a plumber . . . or a physicist? To make the transition from novice to expert? How is human cognition manifest in everyday worklife?

A fresh set of answers to these questions came in a famous 1989 journal article by John Seeley Brown, Allan Collins, and Paul Duguid, colleagues at the Institute for Research on Learning, in Menlo Park, California. In it they argued that the most important knowledge to performance is tacit, that such knowledge resides within and helps define the relevant "community of practice," and that newcomers become contributing practitioners through rites of entry they term "legitimate peripheral participation."

What this last piece of argot means is that you "gotta be there" to learn the most important parts of any job. You don't become a football player, for example, by memorizing the rules and playbook . . . the important knowledge is tacit, it resides in practice; you learn the sport by getting out there on the field with experienced players and doing the thing, over and again. The same, they claim, is true for any craft or profession. You're not suddenly a physicist because you've memorized the for-

Important knowledge cannot be abstracted from the situations in which it is learned and used; knowledge is ever a part of a particular activity, context, and culture.

• •

mulas in a textbook; the community of practice called physics consists of expert practitioners who have their own, internal rules and store of tacit knowledge, an unwritten, sixth sense that tells them what constitutes an interesting question, a good experiment, or a viable theory. Book knowledge has a role, but it's only part of the story: The most important learning is always "situated in practice."

The "learning by doing" aspects of this, you'll sense, hearken back to John Dewey, and indeed the "situated learning" insight has epistemological dimensions. Schools and colleges proceed on the belief that some mix of facts and conceptual representation constitutes best preparation for life's work; indeed, the "merely practical" (and the community itself) are held at arm's length, if not in disdain, by academics. To Brown, Collins, and Duguid, however, important knowledge cannot be abstracted from the situations in which it is learned and used; knowledge is ever a part of a particular activity, context, and culture. In effect, they propose an epistemology of knowledge that puts activity and perception *before* conceptual representation — not the other way around, as it is in classrooms.

One source for this argument comes from findings that student-newcomers to the workplace want to solve problems by reasoning from laws . . . they hearken to the text. Experienced workers, on the other hand, reason from stories — there's a whole set of "narratives" at play in any workplace that allow people to pass on information, share discoveries, and know how things really get done. Experts also draw on stories but they reason with causal models, which they are always testing and refining. Students are trained to produce right answers with fixed meanings; experienced workers and experts produce

We could say that deep learning is requisite to a student's movement from knowledge to understanding, and certainly to any recasting of the mental models he or she uses to view the world.

• •

negotiated meaning and socially constructed understanding.

To enact their vision of how important learning occurs, Brown, Collins, and Duguid propose "cognitive apprenticeships" that will "enculturate students into authentic practices through activity and social interaction" and that support "learning in a domain by enabling students to acquire, develop, and use cognitive tools in authentic domain activity." The authors think the key to more powerful learning lies in building connections *between* learners and *to* the workplace.

There is a profound critique of schooling and academic life, of course, in the situated learning thesis. Not all of it, though, is at odds with practices in higher education. The upper reaches of graduate education (at its best) constitute a form of cognitive apprenticeship: Doctoral students undertake "legitimate peripheral participation" for entry into a community of practice. Situated learning has *not* been advanced as a new approach to teaching or curriculum; it simply attempts to describe how powerful, important learning occurs. Nevertheless, I think its proponents would think well of collegiate practices such as undergraduate research and internships, and of pedagogies such as collaborative learning, problem-based learning, and service-learning.

STUDIES OF STUDENTS

As I said earlier, one way of looking at the American literatures on "teaching and learning" is that they are mostly about teaching, and teachers. In Europe, on the other hand, perhaps because researchers have been loathe to intrude on the lecture halls or send questionnaires to Herr Doktor Professor, there's been a

far greater emphasis on studies of students . . . ethnographic inquiries into how they study, how they approach the taking of courses and doing of assignments, how students approach exams, and so on.

In 1976, two Swedish investigators, Ference Marton and Roger Säljö, published the first of what since has become a stream of studies on student approaches to study. What they reported was that Swedish university students time and again did not get the point of what they were studying "simply because they were not looking for it." What were they doing? Cramming facts into their heads. Why were they doing that? Because they knew that's what they'd be tested for. So what was missed? The *meaning* of the texts they studied, and (especially) how those texts might relate to their own thinking about the world. In Marton and Säljö's observations, most students focused on short-term memorization of facts, formulas, and concepts — as their instructors seemed to ask; the traditional teaching they encountered prompted superficial forms of engagement with subject matter, a "surface" approach to learning.

Only a small percentage of students, Marton and Säljö found, either by disposition or by the demands of the course, undertook what the researchers called a "deep" approach to learning, in which students seek meaning in study, reflect on what they read and hear, and undertake to create (or re-create) their personal understanding of things. Relating this concept to issues raised earlier, we could say that deep learning is requisite to a student's movement from knowledge to understanding, and certainly to any recasting of the mental models he or she uses to view the world.

In 1982, Scotland's Noel Entwhistle replicated these studies with British university students, finding that some 90 percent of the studying going on was of the surface variety. These studies have since been replicated in Canada and Australia, with basically the same findings. To my knowledge, there's been no parallel inquiry in the United States. (One could guess the result.)

Provocative findings have emerged as this line of research was elaborated. One is that when the same instruments are deployed across the high school and college years, there is a steady falling off in deep approaches to learning as students progress up the educational ladder — a depressing finding, indeed. (As W. Edwards Deming used to preach, every school in time will drive the joy from learning.) The second finding is that the same student will take a surface approach in some courses, a deep in another . . . short-term memorization in science, for example, but simultaneous deep engagement with a particular literature course. This latter finding has led researchers to suspect that the approach students take is more a function of instructor demand than of student disposition. Indeed, Australian scholar Paul Ramsden has been able to identify characteristics of courses in which students take a surface approach to learning: The courses obsess over coverage; the huge amount of material they cram in precludes opportunity to pursue topics in depth; students have little choice about what and how to study; and such courses have a threatening, anxiety-riddled instructional and examining environment.

In a latest twist, Entwhistle last year published findings showing that anxiety, fear of failure, and low self-esteem are associated with surface approaches to learning. Further, students are more likely to engage in active forms of learning when they believe that their own effort, rather than external factors beyond their control, determines success. He urges university faculty to build up students' sense of control over their work and get them to exercise responsibility for their own learning.

Let me add that the "deep and surface" line of inquiry posits not two, polar-opposite traits but a continuum of behaviors. Nor should it be taken as denigration of "mere facts." When facts become the be-all and end-all of education, of course we're all in trouble. But a sound base of available knowledge, indeed of socially shared knowledge, is an indispensable platform for shared work and democratic living. In light of this, Entwhistle now talks of "knowledge seekers" and "understanding seekers," with good parts of the former (knowing what or how) necessary to the latter (knowing why).

As you sense, I find this whole line of inquiry provocative. I think the language of deep and surface learning is highly useful . . . preferable, even, to U.S. locutions such as "active vs. passive learning." "Active learning" has the ring of a slogan; "passive learning" is an oxymoron. In contrast, the deep vs. surface formulation is evocative; it captures something important; the words say what they mean. We'd be on a right track if we set as our aim deep experiences of learning for every student in every course.

If "deep vs. surface" as a concept has yet to take hold among researchers here, the phenomenon of superficial approach to task, and of what to do about it, has indeed attracted the attention of American psychologists. Let me mention two recent books on the theme, then a transnational study.

The first is a book that appeared this April, *The Power of Mindful Learning,* by Harvard psychologist Ellen Langer. Like Marton and Säljö, she notices that even the best student may produce right answers but fail utterly to get their point or meaning; like Ramsden, she's keen to the dangers of rote learning, canned assignments, and hurried coverage. The mindless learner, in effect, is on autopilot. Though Langer's book isn't directed at teachers, it is so masterful in adducing insight from a series of small, telling experiments that any teacher will find lots to chew on. Mindfulness, in her view, is promoted by the continuous creation of new categories, openness to new information, and an implicit awareness of more than one perspective. I was reminded by her book, too, of the importance of student choice, of control over task, to ownership of academic assignments and thoughtful engagement with subject.

A different slant on these matters is offered by Chicago psychologist Mihaly Csikszentmihalyi, author of the best-selling books *Flow* and *Creativity*. Csikszentmihalyi uses "flow" as a metaphor to describe the sense of effortless action we feel in times of peak action, moments when heart, will, and mind are as one in an activity . . . that time when our tennis serve was really grooved, or when we lost ourself at the easel or in our garden, or when we got a terrific piece of work done against an impossible deadline. Flow happens, he says, when there's a clear set of goals requiring an appropriate response; when feedback is immediate; and when a person's skills are fully involved in overcoming a challenge that's high but manageable . . . when these three conditions are met, attention to task becomes ordered and fully engaged.

In *Finding Flow,* just out this year, Csikszentmihalyi presents data on how often and where people in the United States and other countries experience flow . . . not often in school, it seems. Why not? we might well ask ourselves.

Then there is the Third International Mathematics and Science Study (TIMSS), perhaps the single largest endeavor in the history of educational research: tens of millions of dollars for parallel studies and testing in some 50 countries, 498 curricula and 628 textbooks analyzed, all in search of cross-national insights about science and math learning in schools. The first TIMSS report, we may note with interest, is called "Characterizing Pedagogical Flow," and you may recall the headline that resulted last year, "Japanese Outdo U.S. Kids in Math." But now the more fine-grained analyses are coming forth, and the story isn't what we may have imagined. That is, Japanese eighth graders do *not* do better because of better-prepared teachers, smaller classes, a longer school year, less TV, and more homework. The differences trace right to the classroom, where the learning goals are clear, the topics per year are few but treated in depth, and where students learn to understand and apply through real-world problem solving and verbalization for meaning. In U.S. schools, by contrast, learning goals are diffuse, coverage is king (30-35 topics a year vs. 6-10 in Japan), textbooks get fatter by the year, and everything has to be taught and retaught again . . . a picture we know all too well in American colleges.

A third TIMSS volume is now out ("A Splintered Vision"), with explicit recommendations for mathematics educators that have resonance across disciplines:

● Focus on powerful, central ideas and capacities.

● Pursue greater depth, so content has a chance to be meaningful, organized, and linked to the student's other ideas, and to produce insight and intuition rather than rote performance.

● Provide rigorous, powerful, meaningful content-producing learning that lasts.

Earlier I observed, perhaps cryptically, that 20th-century social science busied itself proving what philosophers knew right along. I observe here that most of the findings and comment in TIMSS can be found in Whitehead's *The Aims of Education,* published in 1929.

ARCHAEOLOGY

In my search for new literatures on learning, it came as a surprise to me that archaeologists were weighing in on the matter. I'd lost track of developments in that discipline. I didn't know, among other things, that archeologists have developed quite elaborate databases encompassing every prehistoric skull found around the world, with data on its characteristics and on the surround of artifacts found with it; and that from these data it was possible to construct hypotheses not only about how earlier humans lived but about the capabilities of thought apparently available to them.

My text for this section is a wonderful book that appeared last fall, Steven Mithen's *The*

Prehistory of the Mind. Mithen is a brilliant, thirty-something field-worker and theorist at the University of Reading. He works his artifacts like a detective. From them he adduces that our earliest ancestors, several million years ago, seemed to have had only a small, "general" intelligence necessary for basic survival and functioning . . . something possibly higher than but not unlike what we find in apes today. Much later — say, two million years ago — more specialized intelligences started to develop: first a social intelligence, then technical and natural history intelligences, and later a language intelligence. The key "finding," however, is that these were quite separate intelligences, working separately from one another. What early humans found it difficult to do, for example, was to verbalize about the improvement of a tool for an intended use in hunting . . . a conversation, you'll see, that would require fluid access to several domains of intelligence . . . and the impossibility of which explains why a basic handful of tools remained unchanged for a million years at a time. The big breakthroughs of 30,000 to 60,000 years ago — agriculture, religion, art — were to Mithen prompted by a cognitive breakthrough in which the separate "side chapels" of intelligence became accessible to one another, creating a new "cathedral-like" modern brain in which thinking across domains became possible.

I don't want to overdo the Mithen thesis; it is bold, but also a leap, and much at the mercy of new evidence. I report it in the spirit of showing, again, that there are intriguing new ways of looking at learning. I recommend Mithen's book because the subject is fascinating, the writing accessible; the extended footnotes are a treasure trove of leads to related research in a dozen fields. Mithen's concept of a "modular" mind fits well with the "multiple intelligences" postulated by Howard Gardner and Robert Sternberg. Indeed, as you may know, Gardner recently embraced an eighth intelligence, a natural history one, that happens to be a main emphasis in Mithen's thesis.

Csikszentmihalyi presents data on how often and where people in the United States and other countries experience flow . . . not often in school, it seems. Why not? we might well ask ourselves.

● ●

Let me call your attention to another new book, published in 1995 but just out in paper, called *Lessons From an Optical Illusion,* by psychiatrist Edward Hundert, of the Harvard Medical School. Hundert's book is valuable because it weaves the philosophic with the neuroscientific. It considers enduring epistemological questions such as those we began with — What is knowledge? How do humans know? How does the self discover and construct the world? What is the contribution of nature and nurture? What is the mind's relationship between thoughts and things? — and takes the reader through history's conversation about these matters: from Plato and Aristotle to Descartes, up through Locke, Hume, Kant, and Hegel to Wittgenstein and Russell, and on to moderns such as Hilary Putnam and W.V. Quine. Hundert then tours psycho-biological literatures relevant to the question, spending a lot of time on Freud and Piaget, dipping into linguistics, genetics, and artificial intelligence, and laying out the latest insights from brain science. I do bare justice to a learned (and witty) treatise when I tell you that a key conclusion in the philosophers' running conversation — the intersubjectivity of knowledge — coincides remarkably with scientists' emerging understanding of how the brain functions.

There's more to the book than this, let me say, and plenty to argue with, too; when it comes to learning, though, we're all too short on synthesis, so this author's "lessons" are appreciated. I must have marked this book in *ein hundert* places. On the nature vs. nurture debate, for example, Hundert explains that heredity and environment both turn out to be more determinative than we imagined, then cites Gregory Kimball's observation that ask-

Good teachers, like "reflective practitioners" in other professions, constantly test, adjust, and reframe their models of practice on the basis of experience and reflection.

● ●

ing which is more important "is like asking whether the areas of rectangles are determined by their height or their width."

WHAT GOOD TEACHERS KNOW

To Anton Checkov, the artist "observes, selects, guesses, and synthesizes." I claim no "art" for this paper, but it *has* been selective and open to a second-guess. There's so much more to add: about "intelligence," for example, or gender-based and non-Western ways of knowing. Let me press on, though, to Checkov's fourth charge, synthesis.

In the interests of synthesis, I introduce a still-further way of looking at learning, this from a new breed of researchers working in K-12 settings in search of a "wisdom of practice," that is, for what best teachers in real classrooms do with actual students. The basic idea here is that good teachers, like "reflective practitioners" in other professions, constantly test, adjust, and reframe their models of practice on the basis of experience and reflection . . . study what they do, and you'll create new knowledge for effective practice more widely.

But how might the "craft knowledge" of teachers stand in summary of the neuroscientific and related findings recounted in this paper? It can't fully, of course. Yet the two *ought* to be similar and close in spirit, since (as noted earlier) every perceptive teacher is in fact an observer of brain functioning, ever testing and adjusting on the basis of what works with students. In fact, I'd be suspicious of any neuroscientific theory of teaching that was much at variance with what best teachers already knew and did.

All of this is by way of introducing an exercise I conducted with university faculty earlier

this year that attempted to capture a "wisdom of practice" out of the "powerful pedagogies" that have sprung up on campus in recent years. You know these pedagogies — some old, some new, all of them with a following, some of them with a research basis:

● collaborative learning
● cooperative learning
● problem-based learning
● service-learning
● case-method teaching
● peer-based methods
● undergraduate research
● senior capstones
● portfolios
● journals
● multicultural learning
● leadership training

Virtually all of these approaches were fashioned by classroom teachers as a response to real problems with real students; they weren't made up by researchers. So the question becomes, What are the common (if tacit) assumptions these pedagogies make about learning? Looking at the bunch of them, I asked in the exercise, What can we infer about their view of how students learn? What trees do they bark up in common?

The answers were these: The more a teacher can emphasize . . .

● learner independence and choice
● intrinsic motivators and natural curiosity
● rich, timely, usable feedback
● coupled with occasions for reflection *and*
● active involvement in real-world tasks
● emphasizing higher-order abilities done with other people in high-challenge, low-threat environments that provide for practice and reinforcement

. . . the greater the chances he or she will realize the deep learning that makes a difference in student lives.

IN SUM: CYCLES OF LEARNING

The topic of this conference is assessment and quality. How might all this talk about learning color the way we think about those topics?

Most of you will be familiar with David Kolb's "learning cycle," which he introduced in the early 1980s. It's a diagram with arrows around a circle, showing that learning occurs when an act or experience is followed by feedback, which is then reflected on, leading to new understanding, and from there to revised action. In a lifelong, continuous learner, that cycle — act, feedback, reflection, act again — is recursive and never-ending.

Kolb's model, of course, doesn't capture the whole of learning . . . it doesn't by itself get into the kind of "double loop" learning that Chris Argyris showed as necessary for the transformation of mental models, for example. That said, the model nonetheless captures an important insight about learning as a *process*.

To elaborate with an example, I doubt anybody will ask me to give this presentation again. Nevertheless, if I had that chance and wanted to do it better, what I would need is feedback, which would have to be concrete, usable, and credible, from parties or sources I trusted. But feedback alone does not change behavior, a point proved by a hundred studies. What I'd need to do is to engage that feedback, to reflect upon it; and the most powerful kind of reflection I could do would be with other people, because that broadens the wisdom, sharpens judgment, and enhances my commitment. Even there the cycle doesn't stop, because I need the intent and resolve to improve, to use my new understanding in that next presentation. The whole aim of the cycle, then, is Ted's *learning*, that the second time around I'll be smarter and better at this talk.

Kolb's learning cycle is an interesting, persuasive representation of individual learning. It is also a representation of assessment itself.

Assessment is a process in which rich, usable, credible *feedback* from an act — of teaching or curriculum — comes to be *reflected* upon by an academic community, and then is *acted* on by that community — a department or college — within its commitment to get

smarter and better at what it does.

All of which is to say, assessment is more than data gathering. It also encompasses essential functions of meaning-making, action, and commitment to improve. Absent any of these elements, the doing of assessment becomes hollow. When you go to an assessment session at this conference and hear a presenter say, "We did this great study . . . now we're figuring out how to disseminate it," you know something is wrong. What's wrong is that the community was left out. Assessment as learning is not a third-party research project or someone's questionnaire; it is a community effort or nothing, driven by a faculty's own commitment to reflect, judge, and improve.

Kolb's learning cycle was conceived with *individual* learning in mind. But how does an *organization* learn? How does my department or college get smarter and better over time at prompting appropriate learning in students?

And the answer is, *we* learn as *I* learn. That is, a faculty gets smarter and better at its tasks by systematically collecting feedback, reflecting on it, and using the resulting understanding to enact next cycles of work.

Those of you with a background in quality management (CQI) will immediately get the point. Kolb's cycle is quite the same thing as the "plan, do, check, act" cycle of continuous improvement developed by Walter Shewhart at Bell Labs in the late 1920s . . . different words, same idea. (Shewhart, by the way, knew John Dewey, the intellectual father of so many of the ideas in this paper and in whose writing you'll find the idea of cycles of learning. Dewey, I'm told, got the idea from an essay written in 1904 by philosopher Charles Sanders Peirce, Dewey's predecessor in pragmatism.)

All of quality management's injunctions, as Deming and Peter Senge have pointed out, are on behalf of organizational learning. A key element to continuous improvement is the "systematic gathering, interpretation, and use of information for purposes of improvement." In academic settings, that statement also defines assessment. Thus, I say to the quality-management proponents in this audience: Think assessment. And to the assessors here: Think continuous improvement. CQI and assessment are alike in this regard: They are acts of learning in themselves, and the key to prompting the deep learning we want for the students we serve. ◆

BIBLIOGRAPHY

Abbott, John. *Synthesis.* Washington, DC: 21st Century Learning Initiative, 1997. (For an extended bibliography, visit the website at *www.21learn.org.*)

A Private Universe. (Video). Harvard Smithsonian Center for Astrophysics, 1987. (Distributed by the Annenberg/CPB Project, Washington, DC, and by Anker Publishing Co., Bolton, MA.)

Brown, G., J. Bull, and M. Pendlebury. *Assessing Student Learning in Higher Education.* London: Routledge, 1997.

Brown, J.S., A. Collins, and P. Duguid. "Situated Cognition and the Culture of Learning." *Educational Researcher,* vol. 18, no. 1 (1989): 32-42. (See also a special issue of *Educational Technology,* March 1993.)

Bruner, J.S. *Toward a Theory of Instruction.* New York: Norton, 1966.

Caine, Renate N. and Caine, G. *Making Connections: Teaching and the Human Brain.* Reading: Addison-Wesley, 1994.

Csikszentmihalyi, Mihaly. *Finding Flow: The Psychology of Engagement With Everyday Life.* New York: Basic Books, 1997.

Dewey, J. *How We Think.* Boston: Heath, 1933.

Eble, K. *The Craft of Teaching.* San Francisco: Jossey-Bass, 1988.

Edelman, G.M. *Bright Air, Brilliant Fire.* New York: HarperCollins, 1992.

Entwhistle, N. "Motivational Factors in Students' Approach to Learning." *Learning Strategies and Learning Styles,* edited by R. Schmeck. New York: Plenum Press, 1996.

———, and P. Ramsden. *Understanding Student Learning.* London: Croom Helm, 1983.

Goleman, Daniel. *Emotional Intelligence: Why it Can Matter More Than IQ.* New York: Bantam Books, 1995.

Hake, R.R. "Interactive Engagement vs. Traditional Methods: A Six Thousand Student Survey of Mechanics Test Data for Introductory Physics Courses." *American Journal of Physics* (in press).

Highet, G. *The Art of Teaching.* New York: Knopf, 1950.

Hundert, E.M. *Lessons From an Optical Illusion.* Cambridge: Harvard University Press, 1995.

Kolb, D.A. *Experiential Learning: Experience as the Source of Learning and Development.* Englewood Cliffs, NJ: Prentice-Hall, 1984.

Kotulak, R. *Inside the Brain: Revolutionary Discoveries of How the Mind Works.* Kansas City, MO: Andrews and McMeel, 1996.

Langer, E. *The Power of Mindful Learning.* New York: Addison-Wesley, 1997.

Lave, Jean, and Wenger, E. *Situated Learning: Legitimate Peripheral Participation.* New York: Cambridge University Press, 1991.

Marton, F., and R. Säljö. "On Qualitative

Differences in Learning: 1. Outcome and Process. *British Journal of Educational Psychology,* 46(1976): 4-11. (See also *National Teaching & Learning Forum,* vol. 5, no. 1 (1995): 1-4.)

Mithen, Steven. *The Prehistory of the Mind.* London, Thames and Hudson: 1996.

Palmer, P. *The Courage to Teach.* San Francisco: Jossey-Bass, in press.

Ramsden, P. *Learning to Teach in Higher Education.* London: Routledge, 1992.

Senge, P. *The Fifth Discipline: The Art and Practice of the Learning Organization.* New York: Doubleday, 1990.

Shulman, L. "Knowledge and Teaching: Foundations of the New Reform." *Harvard Educational Review,* vol. 57, no. 1 (1986): 1-22.

Sylwester, R. *A Celebration of Neurons: An Educator's Guide to the Human Brain.* Alexandria, VA: Association for Supervision and Curriculum Development, 1995.

Third International Mathematics and Science Study. Successive Reports from Kluwar Academic Publishers, Boston/Dordrecht/London. (See also the website *nces.ed.gov/timss/ index.html.*)

Whitehead, A.N. *The Aims of Education.* New York: Macmillan, 1929.

Theodore J. Marchese is vice president of the American Association for Higher Education, One Dupont Circle, Suite 360, Washington, DC 20036-1110, tmarches@aahe.org.

DATE DUE

Demco, Inc. 38-293